Crafting a Business

Make Money Doing What You Love

* Kathie Fitzgerald

HEARST BOOKS
A division of Sterling Publishing Co., Inc.

New York / London
www.sterlingpublishing.com

Library of Congress
Cataloging-in-Publication Data

Fitzgerald, Kathie.
  Country living : crafting a business: make
      money doing what you love /
      Kathie Fitzgerald.
    p. cm.
  Includes index.
  ISBN-13: 978-1-58816-626-5
  ISBN-10: 1-58816-626-0
  1. New business enterprises--United States-
-Management. 2. Women-owned business
enterprises--United States--Management. 3.
Businesswomen--United States. I. Title.
  HD62.5.F5343 2007
  745.5068--dc22
                              2006035831

10 9 8 7 6 5 4 3

Published by Hearst Books
A Division of Sterling Publishing Co., Inc.
387 Park Avenue South
New York, NY 10016

Country Living and Hearst Books are
trademarks of Hearst Communications, Inc.

www.countryliving.com
For information about custom editions,
special sales, premium and corporate
purchases, please contact Sterling Special
Sales Department at 800-805-5489 or
specialsales@sterlingpublishing.com.

Distributed in Canada
by Sterling Publishing
c/o Canadian Manda Group
165 Dufferin Street
Toronto, Ontario, Canada M6K 3H6

Distributed in Australia by Capricorn Link
(Australia) Pty. Ltd.
P.O. Box 704, Windsor, NSW 2756
Australia

Manufactured in China

Sterling ISBN 978-1-58816-626-5

Contents ✳

* Foreword

HONORING WOMEN WHO HAVE SUCCESSFULLY STARTED BUSINESSES based on their personal passions has long been an integral part of *Country Living*. We have always sought these women and shared their stories. We meet them at trade shows, antiques fairs, flea markets, crafts shows, holiday sales, and at unique shops and studios that catch our eye wherever we travel. In 2006 we began two annual *Country Living* Women Entrepreneurs traditions: an issue with a special section profiling eight or nine of these inspiring creative businesswomen and our Celebration of Creativity, a one-day seminar in Chicago where you may come to hear, meet, and learn from women in the business of doing what they love.

Each business is different, each story unique, and each has something compelling and valuable to say. *Crafting a Business* allows us to gather many more stories in one place than we can in a single issue of the magazine, and I'm thrilled to think that with this collection, women who aspire to starting a business have a resource that resonates with diverse perspectives and offers practical advice for how to begin as well. As you read, you'll find a common thread: each profiled woman did her homework, trusted herself, and embraced her personal passion.

Looking through these pages I am reminded that I never cease to be amazed, not only by the creativity and passion, but by the flexibility, resilience, and sense of purpose with which these women conduct their enterprises. Most of them began their business with a clever idea, lots of passion, and little, if any, business training. How lucky we are that they possess such talent, spirit, and drive. They give us the opportunity to admire, learn from, and emulate their success—and to acquire and enjoy their work as well.

Nancy Mernit Soriano
Editor in Chief, *Country Living*

Introduction ✳

CREATIVITY—USING THE IMAGINATION TO CREATE SOMETHING NEW— is an innate human trait. It is one that many of us would love to fully develop, but all too often, due to the pressures of life or self-doubt, we put it aside. So meeting those who have overcome obstacles and realized their dream of living a creative life is inspiring because it poses the possibility that we can do the same. "I wish I could do what you do," we say to them. "How on earth did you do it?"

This book provides the answer. It tells how women of different ages and backgrounds came to live their dreams as artists and entrepreneurs. Look to them as models and mentors as you use this handbook to reshape your own life.

At the heart of the book are profiles of more than twenty-five women, grouped roughly by the scope of their businesses: *artisans* who make individual items and sell them directly to the public; *shop owners*, some of whom are craftswomen and some not, but all of whom own a retail store; *designer/producers*, whose enterprises involve the mass-production, licensing, and wholesaling of their work; and *service providers*, who sell their skills and expertise. As it happens, many of these talented women belong in more than one of these categories, but we've placed them in the one that corresponds most closely to the focus of their business. The second part of the book is a workshop devoted to the practical considerations of starting and running a business. At the end are resources for starting your own creative journey.

As you read, focus on what these seemingly disparate women have in common: They are all risk takers and decision makers who know that creativity doesn't just happen by itself but requires hard work. Each realized that in order to pursue her passion, she had to become a savvy businesswoman. All have learned to ask for help and to offer it.

As each featured entrepreneur will tell you, the most important decision is the one you make to begin!

ARTISANS

Denise K. H. Carpentier

Liz Alpert Fay

Gloria Lombard

Elisa Strauss

Phyllis Leck

SHOP OWNERS

Denise Allen

Hannah Gray

Michelle Joy

Kaari Meng

Cozbi A. Cabrera

*Nurturing
Your Creativity*

Profiles of Success

DESIGNER/PRODUCERS

Amy Butler

Vicki Mote Bodwell

Anna Corba

Nyakio Kamoche Grieco

Julie Dobies

Crispina ffrench

Marilyn Lysohir

Lori Mitchell

Lisa Norris

Barbara Schriber

Jane Zaccaria

Amie Sikes, Jolie Sikes-Smith &
Janie Sikes

SERVICE PROVIDERS

Judy Godwin

Marcia Gottlieb, ASID

Marki McMillan &
Rae Lynn White

Lucinda Rooney

Kate Shifrin

Maurrie Sussman

* Denise K. H. Carpentier

PEARLWARE POTTER

Averill Park, New York

It seems only natural that poly-chrome pearlware potter Denise Carpentier, who exhibits her exquisitely painted work on the fine-crafts show circuit and creates reproductions for museums, lives and works at Eastfield Village, a late-eighteenth century village outside Albany, New York, in a house that husband Don has been reconstructing for more than forty years. It's also not sur-prising that her paints, brushes, and palette share space in her under-the-eaves attic work area with a sewing machine and cut-ting table for the costuming she does for the local theater. What is astonishing is that Denise, a trained physical therapist, never even handled a paintbrush until daughter Hannah was born eighteen years ago and is almost completely self-taught.

❋ TRADE SECRETS

Denise Carpentier has been ardent in pursuing the skills necessary for a master crafts artist and has been rewarded by seeing her delicate, variegated reproductions appear in museums and private collections. She decided to keep her operation retail in order to maintain control of her prices, making them affordable to a broader market. She believes that while luck and publicity play a role, it is old-fashioned hard work that builds a career.

"I'M VERY PASSIONATE ABOUT MY WORK and about what I do in the theater. It's just that when I feel that way, it's hard to stop. I loved my job as a therapist, but the kind of energy I put into it left nothing for my children, and that was important to me. After my daughter was born I just did not want to go back. Don was teaching himself how to make mochaware at the time and challenged me to paint, and that's where it started. Then one of the curators from Old Sturbridge Village saw some of the things I was working on and asked if they sent me pictures or shards, could I copy them? I did, and when they paid me for them I thought, 'Wow, I can make money doing this!'

"After a while I started making the pieces from start to finish. I started doing just museum work, but you can get really hungry depending on a museum. I've done all sorts of things: African violet pots, Christmas ornaments because I love Christmas. People say, 'I love this pattern, can you put it on some plates for me?' and I say, 'Sure.' It just goes on. I started with retail crafts shows, and I'm still retail. I don't do wholesale so I can do what I want, price things as I want. There's a quote by Winston Churchill I love, it says, 'What we get, is how we make a living; what we give, is how we make a life.'

"WHEN PEOPLE ASK WHERE I LEARNED, I SAY, 'THE SCHOOL OF TRIAL AND ERROR.' One day early on, I walked into an art store for brushes, and the guy asked me what kind of brush I wanted, a

"You can learn something in a classroom but when you make a mistake doing it later, you really remember it because it's not just a grade you need, it's your livelihood."

filbert or an angle? I had no idea. You really learn from your mistakes. You can learn something in a classroom and learn it well, but when you do it at home and you make a mistake you really remember it because it's not just a grade you need, it's your livelihood.

"Whatever you want to do, you can do it, barring any disability of course, but you have to really want it. A lot of people say 'Oh, I'd love to do that,' but are they willing to put out the time and energy? Are they willing to really work? Because that's what a lot of it is. When I was in high school I wasn't allowed to take an art course. They said since I was going to college, why waste the teacher's time on someone with no talent. I love telling that story!

"I'm inspired by the emotions I feel when I do a custom piece for a special occasion. When I've made something that brings happiness to someone else, I want to do it again and again."

✳ **HER DREAM** "Lugging fifty pounds of clay around is beginning to wear on my body, and while I will never stop doing this, what I would love to do is teach. I would love to have a bigger space, a studio totally under my control, and have mostly kids come in and learn what I can teach them. They can hang around with me and help or go off on their own and just do their own thing. They don't have to become artisans; there's more to life than making a living."

✳ Liz Alpert Fay

LIZ ALPERT FAY TEXTILES

Sandy Hook, Connecticut

Luckily Liz Alpert Fay discovered rug hooking—the centerpiece of her thriving home business—because the quilting she'd done since art school just wasn't portable enough for an on-the-go mom. Her designs, inspired by her children's drawings, the zinnias in her mother's garden, and even the color of the eggs laid by her chickens, capture the spirit and character of crafts women have created for centuries. Beautiful in themselves but useful, too, Liz's rugs, until just recently, were created smack-dab in the middle of her home. Now one dream is coming true at last: her own studio.

✳ TRADE SECRETS

Liz Alpert Fay adroitly put her art school training to work crafting hand-hooked rugs, meeting the obligations of a busy life and her creative soul. Recognizing and then following her best business route through juried shows led to commissions, which in turn brought both more income and greater satisfaction. The thrill she gets from coming up with a a winning marketing idea has been a surprising self-discovery.

"I SAW A RUG-HOOKING DEMONSTRATION AND—FORGIVE THE PUN—I WAS HOOKED. I'm able to take my hooking with me to soccer games, school events, wherever I need to go. And with rugs, I shifted to doing juried shows. I knew I didn't want to be selling through galleries, as I'd done previously with quilts, because they take such a high percentage of sales, and I wasn't making enough money to turn it into a business. I thought this might be another avenue, and it was. Then I started getting commissions, which I love! Sometimes people will ask me to incorporate a piece of clothing into the rug; it makes a very personal connection.

"It started out slowly. The first couple years that I came back from shows with enough work to keep me going through the winter, I thought, 'Wow, this is great!' I was busy; I was home with my kids and able to make money. Every year I try to make it better. I'm working on a quilt right now, the first one in probably twenty years. Things are coming full circle for me."

The cyclical nature of her business requires that Liz be disciplined, organized, and plan ahead. "When I do a show I have a master list on my computer with all the things I need for my booth. I do shows only in the fall, so I look at my inventory at the end of the holiday season and plan what I need to get done between then and September. I try to get all my commissions and other work done before summer starts, so I can take the summer to create new work."

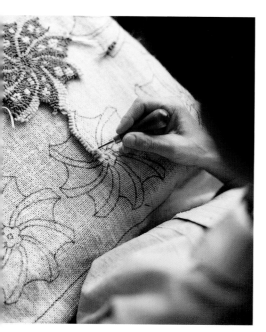

"Sometimes people tell you that you can't do things because maybe they can't do them."

"I'VE FOUND I ENJOY THE BUSI-NESS ASPECTS. Marketing is fascinating, seeing what appeals to people and what gets the best response. It's like cooking: You try a little bit of this and a little bit of that, and see what works." If you are hesitant about starting a business, Liz suggests you "just listen to your heart and don't pay attention to what other people say. Sometimes people tell you that you can't do things because maybe they can't do them, or they think you shouldn't be doing them. Take things one step at a time."

✳ **HER DREAM** "I'm looking forward to giving classes in my studio and having open houses, and I'd love to mentor high-school students. But my dream is a one-person show at a museum."

Gloria Lombard ✳

GLORIA LOMBARD DESIGNS

Johns Island, South Carolina

When Gloria Lombard couldn't find attractive shades to grace the lamps she was selling in her retail antiques shop, she began making her own. Years before, as a single mother, Gloria had taken her father's sensible advice and gone to school at night to learn accounting. But her heart had other ideas, and in 1981, after remarrying, she told her new husband, "Life is too short not to do what you love!" a decision that led her first into antiques and then to her charming handmade French-inspired shades. In turn, a display of the shades at the Brimfield Antiques Show in 2005 drew *Country Living* editors to her booth, and as a result, she was featured as one of their Entrepreneurs of the Year in 2006.

Gloria Lombard has followed

the dictates of the market first

by meeting the demand for

handmade lamp shades and

then by developing a style that

is beautiful as well as profitable

to create. She enjoyed the

support of her family while she

established her business and

insisted on having a studio

where she can let her artistic

spirit fly.

A WEAKNESS IN THE MARKET PRESENTED GLORIA WITH AN OPPORTUNITY. "I never could find decent lamp shades. They were always made of burlap or something just awful. I bought some cut paper shades at an antiques show and started making them. I'd put them on lamps in my booth, and people would say, 'Oh, I don't need that lamp, but I want the shade!' So I realized there was a market for the shades, and I made them for years.

"Then I took a one-day seminar on hand-sewn lamp shades. I began making them with vintage fabric. I got into doing damask shades with monograms, all hand-sewn, but they're so labor intensive, I couldn't keep up with the demand. When my husband retired, I wanted my own business, so I had to make it work. I had pictures from a French magazine of geometric lamp shades with old fabric. They were mainly glued, so they didn't take hours and hours to make. I thought, 'I'm going to try a couple.'

"The bottom line is I went to the Brimfield Antiques Show, and the French lamp shades were a huge hit. I had a big display in my booth with wonderful red lamp shades monogrammed in red or made out of old Turkey-red fabrics. I had red tablecloths hanging up behind them, and it really was a splashy look."

Asked to identify the biggest obstacle she encountered when she established her business, Gloria admits profits were slow to accumulate. "You know, there wasn't always a lot of money. We were raising a family; we had mortgage payments. It's hard sometimes. Luckily I had a husband and son who supported my decision to

"You must have a niche where you can be with whatever turns you on to being creative."

follow my heart; good support makes a tremendous difference."

A PLEASANT WORKSPACE WAS A PRIORITY GLORIA HONORED. "In Maryland I had a space in the basement, but when we built our house in South Carolina, one of my requirements was a workroom. I have the whole back of the second floor. All my fabric is out in piles, arranged by color, so I can find it easily.

"My joy is going to my studio with all that light and color. I'm much more productive now than I've ever been. Not everyone has that option. I made do for years and I was still creative, but you must have a niche of your own, where you can be with whatever turns you on to being creative."

✳ **HER DREAM** "I am very happy. I live where I want to live. I really love my family; it's become even more important to me as I've gotten older."

---

* Elisa Strauss

CONFETTI CAKES

New York, New York

In the last five years Elisa Strauss has built a successful niche business creating custom cakes and is well on her way to building a brand. Yet this dynamo was only twenty-five when she left the fashion world to produce high-end confections of incredible artistry and architecture. If you want your wedding cake to match your dress or would like to throw a party for your pals with a yummy, made-from-scratch, hand-rolled-fondant-and-buttercream cake shaped like a stiletto heel, Elisa's the go-to girl. In addition to writing her own cake-decorating book, she's baked with Martha Stewart, makes frequent appearances on the Food Network, and created a huge replica of an Andy Warhol Brillo box for 800 people at New York's Museum of Modern Art.

TRAINING AS AN ARTIST WAS THE FIRST OF SEV-
ERAL STEPS TOWARD A CREATING A BUSINESS.
"I studied art in college, and this is much more like
producing artwork than running a retail bakery. I
respond to textile designs on couches, carpets,
shoes. If I like the color composition in someone's
outfit, I'll use it on a cake. I encourage brides to do
that, too. If they are having an event with a certain color scheme or want to copy the relief of
their dress—I can do it. You really can do anything.

"I went from college to Ralph Lauren and
then to designing handbags at Frederic Fekkai,
but I knew I wanted my own company. If you
looked in my closet you'd know I'm definitely not
from the fashion world. I started by reading cake-
decorating books, took a few cake-decorating
classes, and went on to pastry school. I went back
to Ralph Lauren as a freelancer, so I'd work half
a day and go to pastry school from one to five
p.m. I moved all the furniture in my little 600
square-foot apartment, so I could work at home
and balance those two careers. I was paid really
well in fashion, and honestly it was hard to give
it up, but people say your career chooses you, and
that's true for me.

"From my fashion experience I understand how
items are built, and my method is the same. If
we're doing a shoe cake, for example, we'll make it
in pieces the same way an actual shoe is made;
that's why it looks so realistic."

✳ **TRADE SECRETS**

Elisa Strauss is the picture of
entrepreneurial fortitude: from
her design training and a simple cake-decorating book have
come astounding confections.
Always looking for publicity,
she scans the masthead of
every publication she reads
and sends off a well-packaged
sample. She's answered the
question of how to grow a
business based on a labor-
intensive product by moving
laterally into publishing and
television.

"Anyone who runs a business has to be a doer."

"I do all my own PR, so I look at magazine mastheads, pick an editor, and send a cake. I had a friend of a friend who wrote for *Time Out* magazine and I got a little blurb in there, and the response from people gave me the confidence to keep going."

Reiterating that her success is the result of persistence and skill as well as talent, Elisa offers a tip for everyone: "Follow up with every single person you send something to and always do what you say you're going to do. People are very busy, so you just have to be persistent in everything." And one for cake decorators especially: "For stacking tiered cakes without ruining the icing, use a palette knife from an art store. They are thinner than offset spatulas and will gently help lay each tier without ruining the icing beneath."

"I JUST HAD A FEELING IF I PUT 150 PERCENT INTO WHATEVER I WAS DOING, IT WOULD SUCCEED. I've seen people who want to start businesses. They take classes in marketing; they take all the right steps, but at the end of the day if you don't have the talent or the will, it doesn't matter. You know, there are dreamers and there are doers. Anyone who runs a business has to be a doer.

✳ **HER DREAM** "My own TV show and products to go with it!"

Phyllis Leck *

VILLAGE WEAVER

Round Pond, Maine

When the snow of a Maine winter drifts against the windows of Phyllis Leck's home studio, she just keeps weaving her charmingly traditional textiles for the home, preparing for the year's crafts show schedule. In the summer months she's there selling her wares along with the work of area artists, including the wrought-iron of husband Andrew. Phyllis was just nineteen when she fell head over heels for Andrew, then a young fisherman, and within three months they married. Alone with her growing family for months at a time, Phyllis taught herself to weave in the quiet hours. Over time, her work has expanded from "country" napkins and place mats to bedspreads and rugs influenced by the colors of the sea.

"I THINK TEXTILES ARE SO MUCH A PART OF THE HOME AND BRING SUCH GRACE TO IT. I believe in the whole family sitting at the table and eating together, and how you dress the table is important." Phyllis's vision for the end-use of her products is a reflection of how they are created: Her work has complemented her husband's and benefited from her children's input.

"We moved to the West Coast for king crab fishing, and when that died we moved back East. Andrew started doing wrought-iron work in the backyard here in Maine when he was fogged in from fishing. He was porgy fishing out of New Harbor, an industry that's now gone, too. I just kept weaving through all the changes. Then I started selling my work, and Andrew became inspired to blacksmith more.

"I'd weave curtain fabric to go with his window hardware, and we'd display it at shows. But now it is changing again, because he is doing more sculptures and railings, and I'm going off with my new line of what I'm calling Harbor Homespuns—bedspreads and rugs.

"When our children were young I involved them in the process. They would play with the yarn and help me select colors. They had a great sense of color, and we enjoyed working together. My sons grew up learning how to weave on the loom, and so did our daughter. They learned to sew, and they all helped in the production of different projects. I had them design things for their rooms, their curtains, their rugs. I try to produce all the textiles we use in our home; we live with my work.

✳ TRADE SECRETS

Phyllis Leck has educated her market to appreciate the way her hand-loomed fabrics enhance the beauty and spirit of a home. She keeps a keen eye on color trends in each of the areas in which she shows her work and has expanded her product lines to meet increased demand. She learned from her mentors that creativity can be incorporated into everyday life.

"I TAUGHT MYSELF BY READING AS MANY BOOKS AS I COULD AND EXPERIMENTING AND PRACTICING. You have to practice, practice, and practice." Phyllis adds, "I think having a garden and trees around you without a lot of noise is important. Being quiet, taking time to sit and be quiet for periods of time allows your mind to create and visualize."

When discussing her training, Phyllis credits peers with fostering her skill and creativity. "A weaver's guild that I joined when I was young helped me learn and furthered my love of weaving. Here were older women who had traveled and investigated weaving around the world, and it had enriched their lives tremendously. They all had families, and that is one thing I always

"You have to practice, practice, and practice."

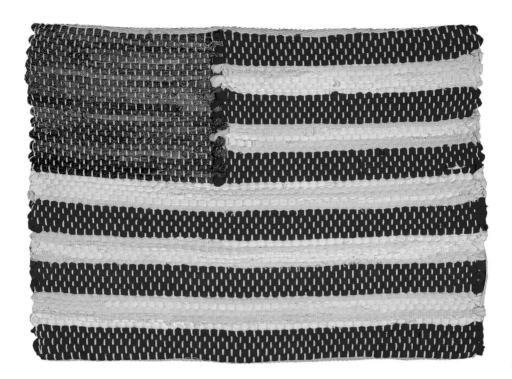

wanted: to have a family, be a wife, be a mother. They showed me how creativity can be—not to be too funny—woven into the fabric of your life."

As a hand weaver of utilitarian textiles, Phyllis has been challenged to educate her market. "I'm surprised at how many people don't understand or appreciate textiles. It is the least appreciated of all the crafts because of the mass production of it now. Everybody loves pottery, they love stained glass, and they love jewelry. But they don't understand what it takes to make fabric. A lot of times people think I just buy the fabric and fringe it, not realizing that each thread has been handled. That has to be explained."

✳ **HER DREAM** "I want to be able to spend time with my family and be successful enough to give to others."

---

* Denise Allen

ALLEN'S 19TH CENTURY GENERAL STORE

Palatine Bridge, New York

Dealing with the loss of her mother, Denise Allen discovered embroidery—the heart of the folk-art tapestries and dolls that now fill her general store and gallery—and the therapeutic power of creativity. Years later, when she also lost her son, she decided the time had come to realize dreams she had harbored since childhood. Leaving the city, she moved to a small, rural town and opened her store. As her business has grown she's added low-cost reproductions of her work, including her own embroidery kit. Denise has known life's trials and tribulations, experiences mirrored in the incredibly expressive faces of her hand-sewn dolls, but her collaged paintings depicting bygone days—which hang in American embassies on three continents—are a celebration of determination and endurance.

SERENDIPITY LED TO SELF-EXPRESSION. "After my mother died I became very depressed, and one day I found myself at Woolworth's in the needlework department. My mother was a self-taught seamstress; she sewed beautiful clothes for us. I bought a little embroidery kit. I took it home, but I couldn't follow the directions—I can't follow the directions from a pattern—so I just figured out how to do the stitching on my own. That was it; I wasn't depressed. I'd found my niche, my calling.

"There I was, doing embroidery, drawing, and stitching, and I thought, 'These would make nice quilts!' So I started cutting them up, adding them to fabrics to make patchworks. Then the dolls: After the first two dolls I made, I knew I had to make these dolls. I had no idea why; they didn't look like much. Often in life you do something, then later you find out why. People said, 'Oh, my God, we love these dolls!' I started to make more dolls, and every time I'd put them out, people would connect with me and tell me their life stories and about their families."

"When I was little, I had recurring dreams of old-fashioned scenes, and when I woke up I'd be very happy. I call them prophetic visions, because I draw those scenes now." For Denise, the connection of past and present has been purposeful and creatively rewarding.

"IF THERE IS SOMETHING I WANT TO DO, I'M THE KIND OF PERSON WHO JUST DOES IT. I'm not letting anything stop me. You've either got it or you haven't." She explains that for her, "It's all

"The one thing you should do is just start. You have to begin somewhere."

been threads, one person leading to another. I was selling my dolls at the Green Flea Market in New York City, where all the museums are. I love that market; you meet all kinds of interesting people there. I met a woman who was a consultant at FIT (Fashion Institute of Technology). She said, 'Denise, you've got potential. You belong in galleries.' I said, 'That sounds good, but how do I do that?' She told me to take a course through AWED (the American Woman's Economic Development Corporation). I took the course, and the last thing I had to do was a presentation on how to market my product, the dolls. So I did my presentation, and as I was getting ready to leave, Joy Mearns, who is a PR person and just happened to be there, stopped me and said, 'Denise, there's somebody you should meet, and I'm going to call

him.' She did, and it was the owner of the gallery that represents me today."

For those who emulate her passion but have yet to pick up their version of her needle and thread, Denise says, "Just begin. Start. I started out with kits. You can learn a little bit from other people. You don't have to take all of their advice, but the one thing you should do is just start. You have to begin somewhere. And just keep going. That's the key."

✳ **HER DREAM** "I want to expand my folk-art gallery, but what I'd really like is to exhibit and sell my work at the Park Avenue Seventh Regiment Armory Shows in New York City."

Hannah Gray ✳

ICEHOUSE GALLERY
NOFO FILM FESTIVAL

Orient, New York

Faced with supporting her children by herself, Hannah Gray began selling her photography at local art shows. The success of that venture encouraged her to open an art gallery and start an independent film festival. On a lifelong mission to reflect the joys and tragedies of the world around her, when the film she'd been using was discontinued, Hannah began to work in the ethereal

platinum printing technique that became her signature (three examples are seen here). As her photographic skill grew, her interests broadened, first to running the gallery in a nearby town on eastern Long Island, and then to organizing the not-for-profit NoFo (North Fork) Film Festival, a year-round program of diverse works submitted by filmmakers from different countries.

YES, YOU CAN . . . IF YOU LET YOURSELF. Hannah explains: "My life has been a litany of people saying 'You can't do that.' At first I had children to take care of, so I started going to out-door art shows to sell my photographs. Unlike the other artists with tents and the proper setup, I had ladders with nails in them for hanging my photo-graphs. As I started to get good and was accepted into juried shows, I went all over Long Island and eventually the United States.

"I went to look for window frames in an old abandoned house because I used them to frame my work. While there, I found a beautiful antique flour can, and when I opened it, it was full of money—thirteen thousand dollars! It had been sitting there since 1928. When it went unclaimed and I recovered from the shock, I said, 'Hey, now I can buy the things I need to look like a real artist in the forum of outdoor art shows.'

"IT NEVER OCCURRED TO ME THEN THAT MY WORK WAS GOOD ENOUGH FOR A GALLERY and I didn't even try to find one. I just went out and tried to sell my work. It started to sell, and I began to make enough money to support myself and my children.

"I was upset about many things going on in the world and that influenced my work. Then I said, 'Wait a minute. This isn't what I want to give to the world anymore.' I just want it to be beautiful. People need hope now. That was a big change for me.

"After photography, I got very engrossed in independent films because the directors were

"When I saw how the the audience was affected by the films, I was very surprised, and I've grown to love that very much."

really addressing the issues that concerned me. I approached a woman who had a gallery in Greenport with the idea of showing films there. We were still working on that when she decided to move to Maine. She said, 'You can have the whole gallery for whatever you want.' So I created a space for showing photography, art, and films. Now, with the NoFo Film Festival, I show films in coffeehouses, performance spaces, and vineyards.

"The idea of opening up a gallery wasn't one I'd had, but I absolutely love the openings, with everybody here networking. At first I didn't know what would happen; I thought film showings would be entertaining events. But when I saw how the people in the audience were affected by the films, I was very surprised, and I've grown to love that very much.

"HOW COULD I SAY ANYTHING BUT 'SHOOT WITH YOUR HEART'?" asks Hannah when queried about words of wisdom she'd like to pass along. "I'd give the same advice that was given to me: Shoot what you really want and just write down what you do: F8 at 250, for example. Certainly don't start with digital. Get a Nikon F2, go out and get 100 rolls of film and just shoot."

She adds, "My house is very important to what I do. Every artist I've ever visited sees their home as part of their work. The house to an artist is just another installation, and that's what mine is. The kids know, 'Watch out, the beds are Mom's installation'!"

✳ **HER DREAM** "My dream is to bring art and film to at-risk kids and someday to work in Africa."

Michelle Joy ✳

PRIMROSE

Somers Point, New Jersey

When a friend offered Michelle Joy a loan to start her own retail florist shop, she took it and ran. After years of having her creativity stifled working for other people in the flower industry, she was brimming with plans. An Irish redhead with the spirit to match, she brought such energy and élan to the effort that she was able to open a second store. While she enjoyed running a growing business, a chain of florist shops just wasn't what she wanted, so when she spotted a rundown old house that she knew she could rehab as a showcase for her floral and interiors styling, she sold the second store and grabbed the house. From there it took only a couple of steps to begin redoing the homes of her customers.

UNIQUE, HANDMADE PROMOTION CAN BE
EXCEPTIONALLY EFFECTIVE AND SURPRIS-
INGLY AFFORDABLE. "I didn't do a lot of advertising for the opening of my shop; I couldn't afford
it," says Michelle. "A 60-second radio commercial
costs $500, so I invested in 250 little bottle plants,
slipped my business card in, and personally deliv-
ered them to all the businesses up and down the
road. I figured for what cost me 90 cents apiece,
people might say, 'Okay, let's give this girl a shot.'
It sat on everybody's counter with my business
card in it; that was how I got my name around.

"Selling the second store gave me the down
payment for my house, and that's how it came
about. My town has a Christmas house tour and I
got on it. Someone from the local newspaper came
through the house tour. I'd only been in the house
three months, and it was still very dilapidated, but
he said to me, 'I have to do a story on you. This
house is amazing.' I said, 'Okay!' That was my first
in. The three-page photo-essay he did on my
house brought me business."

AMBIENCE IS KEY TO THE EXPERIENCE OF
SHOPPING AT PRIMROSE, where the interior
design and floral businesses both thrive. "If you walk
into my store, you won't know you're in a florist's
shop until you go to the back, where you see the big
flower fridge. It's not a typical flower fridge; it's wall-
papered in cabbage roses and has old wood trim. My
counter is made of salvaged windows. People come
in and just meander around with their coffee and
ask, 'Can I just sit down at the table and finish my

✳ **TRADE SECRETS**

Michelle Joy knows that energy
and style can make up for a
small advertising budget and
that on-the-job training trumps
classroom learning. Her lavish
trademark roses are a wedding
standout; they also enhance the
gracefully aged furniture in
her shop, adding to the oh-so
comfortable atmosphere that
beckons people over the
threshold. She's discovered
that, if nurtured, the customer-
designer dynamic is a source of
inspiration for both parties.

"I figured for what cost me 90 cents apiece, people might say, 'Okay, let's give this girl a shot.'"

coffee?' I say, 'Sure, go ahead.' I'm in the back doing three weddings; that's my bread and butter. It's all about getting people in the door and interested."

MICHELLE BEGINS A COMMISSION BY OBSERVING HER CLIENTS. "My customers give me inspiration. When I'm doing someone's wedding I become like a part of the family for more than a year. I'm at their homes, we have dinner together, they ask my opinion, and they give me carte blanche to do something original. The way their house is designed will give me an idea. They'll give me feedback that makes me feel good and I become more inspired."

Asked about advice for would-be floral designers, Michelle says, "Get a job—any job—in a flower shop. Ask if you can work two or three days a week. Ask if they are looking for holiday help. The best way to get your foot in the door is to actually work in a flower shop. That's where you'll learn. Hands-on is the best teacher; it always has been."

✳ **HER DREAM** "I have a whole series of books dying for me to put them together. I want to do a quarterly magazine: summer, spring, winter, and fall. I have it laid out in my mind, from soup to nuts. I know how I want it advertised, marketed. It's all based on exactly how I live my life and run my shop—how to have a better life for less."

---

* Kaari Meng

FRENCH GENERAL

Hollywood, California

French General, Kaari Meng's retail lifestyle atelier—an old, sprawling, Spanish-style house in Hollywood brimming with antique and custom textiles, handmade nostalgic notions, and locally made natural body products—is la crème de la crème resource for aspiring crafters and decorators far and wide. Kaari and her sister had been making regular trips to France for years, coming back with old linen sheets, enamelware, and silver they began selling out of an old barn along the Hudson River. They'd decided to make the huge leap to a store in Manhattan when Kaari was diagnosed with a life-threatening illness. Nonetheless French General was launched in 2000 with fabulous success. Realizing later that it was not what she wanted, Kaari moved everything to California and began retooling.

"Everything that leaves this shop is very personal . . . people buy into my 'eye' and what I'm designing."

Kaari Meng has been unerring in reading her market, taking a successful retail operation and transforming it into a lifestyle brand. She's built trusted relationships with her vendors, all of whom are nearby. She's been perceptive in spotting that it's her hands-on approach to each piece that gives French General its cachet.

A LOVE OF COLLECTING WAS THE IMPETUS FOR IT ALL. Before launching her store, Kaari had been a designer of vintage glass jewelry that sold in top-of-the-line shops. "My jewelry came from my love of collecting old glass, beads, baubles, trims—all the little notions I'd always loved. It was great for me because it was portable. I could move around, make it at home or rent a small studio, and do the trade shows two or three times a year.

"My sister had come to work for me and organize me and we had been kicking around the idea of French General. People really got into what we'd bring back from France, and our barn sales got bigger and bigger. Just when we made a commitment to move to New York City, I became ill. My family moved back East to New York and my dad, my brothers, and my husband renovated the space while my mom and sister and sister-in-law and I got everything ready, which took a while because of my treatment.

"After five years I realized that the retail store we had was getting me down. After what I'd been through it hit me that I had to do exactly what I wanted to do every day; there wasn't really a choice anymore. So we moved to California, where I'm from originally, and took six months to rethink the business.

"WE CAME UP WITH THIS CONCEPT OF A WORK-SPACE THAT WOULD BE OPEN TO THE PUBLIC and serve as an inspiration to the whole crafts and textile notions world. Each room in the house is set up differently. The front room is the textile room,

there's a laundry room where we do all our cleaning of the linens, and there's the creative room in the back, where we have all our classes and put together our notions kits and where I still make jewelry.

"I don't carry anyone else's work. I buy the fabric, but I print my own fabric, too. We pick up the old sheets in France every year; they're dyed with vegetable dye in the Valley. I employ two full-time seamstresses, and we make all the textiles. All my shea butters are made right here in Silver Lake; all our vendors are within two miles. My husband designs the paper line; he

is a master designer. He and I have been partners since we moved out here.

KEEPING YOUR BUSINESS A MANAGEABLE SIZE CAN ENSURE FUTURE GROWTH. "I prefer to do some things myself, my notions kits for example. I believe I understand color better than most employees would, and that holds me back. Everything that leaves this shop is very personal, and a big reason it does leave is because people buy into my 'eye' and what I'm designing."

✳ **HER DREAM** "I love the idea of just taking this French General lifestyle and putting it on a grand scale on a big piece of land—a place to go to for inspiration, maybe for a week or a few days. People could take three crafts classes a day or a seminar on how to run a small business or go out in the field and harvest lavender!"

Cozbi A. Cabrera ✳

COZBI INC.

Brooklyn, New York

Starting with her beautifully cos-
tumed one-of-a-kind handmade
dolls, Cozbi Cabrera opened and
runs a thriving retail business that
now includes children's clothing
and accessories, quilts, and a
women's clothing line for "real
people." But Cozbi was a successful art director at Sony
Records when she discovered a
set of folk-art black dolls at an
antiques show and realized she'd

found her calling. Seeing a void in the marketplace, she set out
to fill it with her *Muñecas*, so-named in honor of her Honduran
heritage, selling her first doll for $65 in 1997. She's gone on to
expand her product line, open her own shop, and illustrate children's books. The women's clothing line has done so well, it has
sustained the operation.

"SO MUCH HAS COME FROM JUST MAKING A DECISION TO DO WHAT I LOVE! I sold a number of dolls at work and began to show them around in shops in the New York area. At that point I didn't even care about placement; I was just looking for a response. I learned that they were, in fact, quite marketable, so I decided to leave my job and devote myself full time to doll making. I did so much hand beading and all this detail work on the dolls that I thought that the more time I was able to give it the more I could get back.

"I'd been doing so many shows and done so well that heading into the last show of the month, I had hardly any dolls to display. Sort of sobbing, I just took what I had and used my quilts to fill the space. Someone saw me there and told the editor of *Martha Stewart Living* TV about this woman who did quilts. The editor came to my house to do a little scouting for quilts, saw the dolls, and got very excited. They did a beautifully produced segment on the dolls, and the response that flooded in from all around the country was absolutely tremendous."

FOR COZBI, NURTURING HER BUSINESS WAS A MATTER OF FOCUS AND COMMITMENT. "I never took a sewing class. I just began. That's how I grew, and also by setting aside time to practice the craft. All the courses in the world are no substitute for the actual doing." She does credit her parents for planting the seeds of her skill, however. "My mother sewed and did a lot of crocheting. My dad also had some very remarkable hand skills; he could literally put anything together."

✳ TRADE SECRETS

Cozbi Cabrera has been clear sighted in her projections, favoring organic growth over more risky methods. Careful financial planning allowed her the time to develop her skills to the requisite levels. Her elaborately hand-sewn dolls and clothes are stunning, but she knows that at the end of the day, it's the bottom line that matters.

"In order to function it's not enough to be creative; the numbers have to work as well."

As her endeavors met with success, she says, "I simply made a commitment to move forward with the business and to grow it and to cultivate it, and from that commitment things started to align themselves. Financially, I had savings that over the course of the years I tapped into, but I also did some hand quilting and general handwork for additional income. It's interesting because you think of yourself as an artist or a craftsperson, but in order to function it's not enough to be creative; the numbers have to work as well."

✳ **HER DREAM** "I love the idea of an atelier, a space where artisans and craftspeople, such as pattern makers, come together. And I do think that there are some core pieces in our clothing line that could be contracted out to a very responsible company. I would like to begin to do a little more wholesale, and I can see a second shop, perhaps in New York City."

---

* Nurturing Your Creativity

Serendipity aside, the refined concept that is key to a thriving business is unlikely to leap full-blown from your brain. It takes time, thought, and experimentation for the germ of an idea to mix with your specific skill or passion and grow into a vision you can articulate clearly and realize as a viable venture. The process is different for everyone. Here are thoughts to get you started.

GIVE YOURSELF ROOM *

Just listen to your heart and don't pay attention to what other people say. • My goal is being in my studio, keeping my hands in beauty. • I'd paint until ten or eleven at night, and I realized it made me come alive. • The more my passion was shaped to my purpose, the more I started living. • I need to be relaxed in order to create. • Give yourself room to experiment, to come up with ideas. It has to be a priority.

LIFE GIVES YOU CLUES *

Meet people. It's amazing how a conversation or even one word can make something click. • They showed me how creativity can be woven into your life. • People say your career chooses you. • Just start something and see where it takes you. • I figured out how to do the stitching. That was it—I'd found my calling. • Be open and watch for the clues that come drifting by. If you ignore them, they disappear.

HONOR YOUR PASSION ✳

Sit down with a piece of paper and a pencil and write down everything you like and can do: This is what I love, this is what inspires me, and this is what gives me courage. • Be quiet; taking time to sit and be quiet for periods of time allows your mind to create and visualize. • My joy is going up to my studio with all that sunlight and color. • For me it's always been 'make something, make something, make something!' • I just want it to be beautiful. People need hope now. • I'm inspired by the emotions I feel when I do a custom piece. • Being able to walk out my kitchen door and cut herbs in this beautiful environment is heaven. • My jewelry came from my love of collecting old glass, beads, baubles, trims—all the different little notions I'd always loved. • What I've always done is saturate myself with places, experiences, books, or environments that make me feel creative.

TRUST YOURSELF ✳

I have a page in my sketchbook, and when I'm feeling all scared and think "This is not going to work," I write down all the good things that have happened. • I think lack of courage is the number-one obstacle. • *Yes* is the magic word. • I just did what I knew and trusted my ability. • Don't ever go below your standards. • After the first two dolls I made, I knew I had to make these dolls. • It comes from somewhere inside of me. I don't know where, but I've learned to trust myself.

STAY FOCUSED ✳

It's easy to get distracted, and it's easy to look over your shoulder. • Be passionate about what you do and be quality oriented. • I have a hard time working in a vacuum, without guidelines. • Just begin and just keep going. That's the key.

* Amy Butler

AMY BUTLER DESIGN

Granville, Ohio

Amy Butler's wonderful passport bag—the first item in her fresh and sassy wholesale sewing-pattern line—was born when, right out of art school, she landed a job in the corporate world in Kansas City, a world she quickly realized was just not for her. She and partner and husband, David—as they do at every twist in life's road—sat down, discussed the situation, and came up with a solution. Amy quit the corporate world, took a part-time job as a receptionist at the design firm where David worked, and began designing her accessory patterns. A move back home to Ohio has allowed her to flourish. She's added fabric designer and book author to her growing list of accomplishments.

Amy Butler hasn't been afraid to be different; her vintage-modern accessory patterns and fabric design readily filled a void in the market. Taking the time to get away and travel revives her creative spirit, and having a true partnership with her spouse is the basis of her personal and professional growth. She's discovered that watching members of your staff blossom can be enormously rewarding.

"I STARTED MAKING A FEW DIFFERENT SIMPLE STYLES OF BAGS AND SELLING THEM to local, then national, shops, slowly gaining confidence," Amy explains. "A friend suggested that I make the patterns and sell them, so I did. Five years ago I took some designs to a spring quilt market in Kansas City, where I had my first booth. No other small pattern companies were doing accessory patterns, and mine were all bags, children's things, and items for the home. I didn't realize I would be so different; I just did what I knew and trusted my ability. I didn't get a lot of distributors right off the bat, but I was approached by one of the top names in the quilt-fabric design industry. She asked, 'Have you ever thought about designing a line of fabrics?' Honest to God, that's been one of my lifelong passions. So that's how I got started.

"I'm a lucky girl because David is such a great partner on every level. A lot of our business plans are created on long walks. We'll just go out, get away from the studio, and come up with terrific solutions or new ideas. Our relationship is always changing, and I think that's why it works, because we're flexible. We've been together twenty-plus years now, so we've learned to see all the road signs, those Stop or Caution signs when something comes up that's not right. Then we know we need to sit down, catch a breath, and rethink it."

EXPLORE AND LEARN FROM THE PEOPLE AND PLACES YOU COME ACROSS—sources of inspiration and growth are everywhere. "When you're

"Let everybody know this is something you need to do and ask that they respect your time and honor it."

starting out," Amy says, "networking is the person down the street bringing you the homemade cherry pie because you just moved in. People find you and you find other people in all kinds of ways. You help each other with ideas, and you're friends for life. You look out for one another. It makes you more confident. You're not out there doing it alone, for one, and you find all kinds of great resources that way. You never know when you are going to need to learn how to go to China to manufacture something or how to hire your first employee.

"Travel is one of my biggest inspirations because we spend so much time just running the day-to-day business. Occasionally we need to get out of our familiar element. I need to be relaxed in order to create. Even just crazy little road trips are great. For example, we rent huge box trucks and pile our friends in and go plant hunting for a weekend."

Amy adds that the route her business has taken has been full of the unexpected: "Watching other people grow. We are what we make, and working with other people is an opportunity to grow on all levels. There's no better way than working with others to decide what is really

right or wrong or what kind of standards you should have. That is probably the most surprising thing for me.

"Make space for being creative in your life. Give yourself room to explore and experiment, to come up with ideas. It has to be a priority, just as important as going to the store and buying groceries every week. Let everybody know this is something you need to do and ask that they respect your time and honor it."

✳ HER DREAM "We're doing it! We're working with a manufacturer here in the United States to actually produce our bags. And I'm working with several companies to license this very cool combination of products I've designed: pillows and accessories, toiletry bags, and items like that. It will expand my brand and introduce me to new markets. It's really exciting."

---

* Vicki Mote Bodwell

THE WARM BISCUIT BEDDING COMPANY

New York, New York

Manufacturer and retailer Vicki Bodwell always wanted to start her own business, and when her friends started complaining about the lack of attractive children's bedding, she thought she might be on to something. With young boys at home, she decided that a catalog and Web site offering great-looking sheets, blankets, and spreads was a natural starting point. Her first catalog was mailed to 25,000 people, and she's now up to two million. She heads a team of designers and artisans, and has added apparel, fabric, bath accessories, and customized furniture to her product line, giving credence to her own motto: "Think big; start small."

"Networking is instrumental; you cannot go
and do it alone."

Vicki Mote Bodwell spotted a
real opening in the market and
leapt into it with her children's
bedding products; her retail
catalog and Web site marketing
approach drove brand identity
and dovetailed with her desire
to be at home with her children
to boot! Terrific publicity
engineered in-house boosted
her mailing list as well as her
self-confidence.

VICKI MAY HAVE STARTED SMALL, BUT SHE WAS SMART ABOUT IT and fortunate in her timing. "In the bedding market it's hard to create a brand," she says. "Since we wanted to create a brand identity, a catalog and Web site enabled us to create a full look and feel exactly the way we wanted it. It turned out to be the right thing to do because we started in 1998, and Pottery Barn Kids came out a year later. They created the market for me and for a lot of other people. I'm a huge believer that competition makes you stronger. As a small company, you have to constantly decide where you are going and what niche you are going to own. Ours is giving average moms a custom look at an affordable price.

"It took about two years before I quit my job in publishing and went to work for my business full time. I was very cautious. I'm a mixture of spontaneity and caution. After I had my second child and was home on maternity leave, breast feeding and answering phones at the same time, I knew I had to focus and choose between my job and my business."

GOOD CONTACTS AS WELL AS GOOD IDEAS WERE CRITICAL for the growth of Warm Biscuit Bedding Company, gaining it notice and helping it weather some growing pains. Vicki notes, "For problem solving, I have a group of friends who are in marketing and I have a group of friends who are in accounting. Networking is instrumental; you cannot go and do it alone. What's interesting about entrepreneurs is that most people want to help the little guy; they really want you to succeed."

She continues, "Like the tortoise and the hare, slow and steady wins the race, but the big break was getting exposure and collecting names. I would say PR was absolutely the pivotal piece of our development. We did it ourselves, and I'm really proud of that. Hiring a PR company is a huge chunk of your budget, and we were concentrating on spending every dime on getting the catalogs out there. We had great mentions in *Country Living* as well as *House & Garden* and *InStyle*; that gave us momentum in gathering names for our mailing list both from the Web site and people calling the toll-free number."

"Several years ago we were trying to grow really fast and aggressively, but unless you have the right systems in place you're not equipped to do that. We hunkered down and restructured the entire operation for the long term.

It was a real learning experience; my husband calls it my MBA!"

To keep your endeavor in forward motion, Vicki urges, "Stay focused. It's easy to get distracted and it's easy to look over your shoulder; as an entrepreneur you're constantly in a state of panic." She adds a tip that works for her: "Women are a remarkable inspiration. My grandmother raised six kids. Whenever I'm having a difficult moment, I turn to her. She's my rock."

✳ **HER DREAM** "A group of design consultants taking our product line directly to customers: hosting parties in their homes showcasing the products and helping other women design their rooms. It's exciting because these consultants could make their own hours, work from home, and do something they're passionate about—it's what got me started."

---

* Anna Corba

FOUND CAT STUDIO

Santa Rosa, California

Living in the rolling vineyards of northern California nourishes Anna Corba's soul and helps fuel the creation of her vintage-inspired handmade home accessories, which she distributes through the large gift shows. An art history major turned painter, she and her husband moved back to California to escape harsh eastern winters only to find the employment scene less than welcoming. In response, Anna went back to her artistic roots, and in a small carriage house behind their home began giving new life to old objects.

fondée en 1797

UPOUY

ourg St-Honoré, 123

PARIS

Eau
de
Toilette

CH. FAY

9, Rue de la Paix
PARIS

PARIS
PRIX-COURANT
DES VINS DE
CHAMPAGNE St-MARC
ET
G. M.

NCE P.

TS

E-BEE
WIND .... .30
THE GRASSHOPPER FAMILY .... .25
MOONBEAM DANCE
GIPSY CAMP .... .30
.... .30

Price complete 75 cents

Anna Corba's heart and hands
put their imprint on every piece
of vintage ephemera leaving
her studio—and that's just
how she likes it. She knows
that while a creative life can
be intoxicating, it requires a
deadline-meeting, day-in-day-
out work ethic to be more than
a hobby.

"I HAVE A QUOTE PINNED UP IN MY STUDIO:
'IDEAS DON'T COME BEFORE YOU WORK.
They come after you start working.' In my case, I'm
lucky enough to have a studio. For some women it
means sitting down at the kitchen table and just
beginning. For many women the question is 'Where
do I start?' If you are reading this book, there is
something in you, some dream, and that's a start."

For Anna, starting meant sitting in her studio,
creating, and then holding an open house. "One
year, for the holidays, I started doing small things
like journals and tags and bottles and candles. I
got together with some friends and opened my
studio doors. People came, and I got a great
response. I got instant feedback on what I was
doing as well as a mailing list. Hearing people's
reactions helped me gain a lot of confidence.

"I took some pictures of my work and of my
studio and I sent them off to *Country Living* and to
Mary Engelbreit's Home Companion, and those
magazines presented my work! As a result of those
two articles, which serendipitously came out in
the same month of that year, I started getting
phone calls from shop owners and from individ-
uals, and I was filling orders."

Anna credits her upbringing with giving her the
confidence to make her own way. "My parents were
not artists. I wasn't trailed around flea markets all
my life or anything like that, but I also was never
told 'That's a silly thing to do. That's an impractical
thing to do.' There was always this nice balance of
'You can make your own decisions' and, 'We trust
you but try to think of the larger picture.'"

"You need to grasp the opportunities when they fall in your lap."

"YOU NEED A WORK ETHIC. THE WHOLE ARTIST RIDE IS A JOB, LIKE ANYTHING ELSE. Yes, it can be very romantic, and the creativity is very intoxicating and seductive, but it's also a job. You need to show up every day in your studio, you need to make those phone calls, and you need to grasp the opportunities when they fall in your lap."

For Anna, it's a job she treasures. "I love the whole organizational process of it. I love organizing all the orders, getting them set in a definable weekly unit. I do everything: all the billing, receiving, and shipping. My husband helps when he can, and I do have a part-time assistant once or twice a week, but it's very small and I keep it that way willingly. I have to meet my deadlines, do what I say I am going to do, and make sure I get paid for it."

Of her training, she says, "I think the degree I got in art history was definitely a great thing to do. But for me it's always been 'make something, make something, make something!' At the end of two weeks, I'd have twenty-four books. At the end of another week I had ten bottles, then sixteen tags. I never thought, 'Oh, I'm going to put on a holiday sale!'

✳ HER DREAM "My dream is truly to keep spending my days in my studio. Whether it's my product line or my artwork or writing and producing more books, as long as it's creative, my goal is being in my studio, keeping my hands in beauty."

Nyakio Kamoche Grieco ✳

NYAKIO BATH & BODY

Los Angeles, California

After seven years spent climbing the Los Angeles entertainment-industry ladder, business school graduate Nyakio Kamoche Grieco turned to her heritage to begin developing and manufacturing a wholesale line of beauty products based on natural ingredients and  age-old secrets. As a little girl, first-generation American Nyakio loved watching her mother prepare the skin-care oils and lotions she'd learned to make growing up in Kenya. Now a new mother with a daughter of her own, Nyakio looks forward to using the fruits of her entrepreneurial efforts to help others, particularly women and girls.

✳ TRADE SECRETS

Nyakio Kamoche Grieco deftly merged her business training and lineage to satisfy the growing demand for natural products; her bath-and-beauty line, with ingredients like pomegrante and sage, subtly echoes the sweet-and-spicy mélange found in some African and Asian cuisines. She's been enterprising in seeking substantial financing while fostering bonds with those she deals with on all levels.

A SOLID BUSINESS PLAN APPEALED TO INVESTORS. "I started researching and assembling family recipes while continuing to work at my job," explains Nyakio. "I went back into my old marketing folder from college and used a business plan I'd done as a model for Nyakio. I started sending the word out that this was something I really believed could work, and a family friend introduced me to a couple of people he thought might be interested. That's when I got investors and financing. About three weeks later, I hired a chemist and began research and development.

"I spent several months in development, testing, and production before I launched. Our turning point came right at my initial launch at Fred Segal here in L.A. Because I had spent a lot of time talking with the employees there in years past, they were very supportive when I launched my line. We also had people from the press at our launch party, and I got a lot of attention from *Women's Wear Daily* and other local publications. The press write-ups really boosted our sales. Obviously it took a while to break even or see a profit. It was probably at the close of year one when I realized that this enterprise could really work and I started adding new things to the line."

MAKE YOUR UNIQUE BACKGROUND OR EXPERIENCE APPEALING TO A BROADER MARKET. "Many of the ingredients I use, like pomegranate and sage diffusers, are indigenous to Africa. I love to base my products on the cuisine, especially that of East Africa, where my family is from. Kenyan

"What you put out there comes back to you!"

food, like Indian food, is often a combination of spicy and sweet. So, applying that concept to my products, I mix fruit with spice: a grapefruit and tarragon combination, pomegranate and sage, or raspberry and basil. I remember the smells growing up, when my mom would make Kenyan food, spicy and sweet at the same time."

Although her business is more corporate than the others in this book, Nyakio's advice to budding entrepreneurs nonetheless comes straight from the heart: "Pay really close attention to the people who come into your life and nurture your relationships. What you put out there comes back to you!"

✳ **HER DREAM** "To raise a happy well-adjusted child! Professionally, I want to expand Nyakio to include a baby line, a line of organic products for expecting moms, which was really hard for me to find when I was pregnant! My long-term goal is to be in a position where I'm able to give back, especially to women and children. I'd like to establish a school in Africa."

✳ Julie Dobies

FINE-ART PAINTER

Chicago, Illinois

The decision to market her luminous and evocative original oil paintings as a retail product line and then sell museum-quality prints both retail and wholesale came easily to Julie Dobies. When she was a little girl she and a friend got their moms to hold "art parties," where their creations took the place of the more conventional Tupperware. During a career as a photo stylist and manager of a Shabby Chic store, she honed her design and business skills, but her spirit wasn't satisfied until she began to paint lush depictions of the flowers she tends in her garden. Then, three years ago, to complete an already rich life, she and her husband adopted a baby girl.

"Two people wanted to buy the same painting; that registered, and I looked into making quality prints."

✳ TRADE SECRETS

Julie Dobies astutely weds her retail background to her gorgeous, peaceful paintings by conceptualizing a product line before she begins and looking continually for new avenues of expansion beyond traditional fine-arts marketing. She knows which aspects of the business she doesn't want to deal with herself. She believes training is great but feels too much of it can remove the artist's essence from her work.

"I'D PAINT UNTIL TEN OR ELEVEN AT NIGHT, AND I REALIZED IT MADE ME COME ALIVE," says Julie of the time she spent taking evening classes while still working fulltime. "I enjoyed my job at Shabby Chic and had a great salary, but it wasn't about having money anymore; it was about having a life. So I decided to take a week off and paint every single day as if it were my job and see how it went. I produced so much work it was phenomenal. Soon after, I had friends over for dinner, and they wanted to buy my paintings! That was the turning point, when I first thought, 'I can do this!'

"My first idea was to show oil paintings as samples for people to order, but I guess it was a little crazy and people didn't get it. So I introduced myself to some of the local merchants where I thought my work would fit in and one of them offered to do a show. At that show two people wanted to buy the same painting; that registered, and I looked into making quality prints. I had everything photographed professionally so it could be produced in all sizes. At first I was doing it myself, but I hated the whole process. I wanted to be a painter, not run a factory.

"I made myself a little marketing kit with images of my work and a letter stating that I wanted to produce art prints and sell them to retail stores, but that I knew I couldn't do it myself. I sent the kit to a vendor I met at a trade show, and he took the line!"

JULIE KEEPS POTENTIAL CLIENTS IN MIND AS SHE DEVELOPS HER LINE, remembering how the customers at Shabby Chic sought art to complement that decorating style. "I often have a marketing idea before I start. For example, I'll plan a line to market in stores along the coast for beach houses, and I'll incorporate the sky and water. As I'm painting, I'll think of titles, or I'll buy an antique frame and paint for that frame. I think my work looks vintage—I joke there's a grandmother inside me trying to get out.

About the drive behind her success, she says, "I have a quote that inspires me. It was used by Nelson Mandela in his inaugural address: 'Our deepest fear is not that we are inadequate. Our deepest fear is that we are powerful beyond measure. It is our light, not our darkness, that most frightens us. It's not just in some of us, it's in everyone.'"

Julie feels anyone wanting to pursue a path similar to hers should

find the quote inspiring. She adds, "Do what you love even if it's only at night. Meet people. It's amazing how a conversation or even one word can make something click. You need some instruction, but not so much it strips away the character of your work. Whoever you are, you are going to be."

✳ **HER DREAM** "I love to cook, and as an artist I see how beautiful food can be. I've thought about incorporating all this into a book: a whole philosophy of design and a cookbook with my paintings. If I could have my dream, I think I would really love to do that, and maybe run a small gallery in some exclusive summer resort area that's open only one month a year."

---

* Crispina ffrench

CRISPINA DESIGN WORKSHOP

Pittsfield, Massachusetts

A true pioneer of repurposing, Crispina ffrench makes plush and funky color-filled rugs, blankets, and pillows—the mainstay of her wholesale accessories company—from recycled clothing. After working her way through a Boston art school selling toy animals, Crispina had a life as an artist and environmentalist in British Columbia all planned out. But when she was accepted by a prestigious local crafts fair—and wrote so many orders that she could barely keep up—her life took a dramatic turn. Twenty years later, she has big-name companies knocking on her door, which just happens to be a renovation-in-progress of a lovely old former New England church that is home to her business and her growing family.

Crispina ffrench has been

agile and seemingly fearless

about seizing opportunities to

develop her business. Her

textiles have a quirky yet

unmistakable identity that is

true to her creative vision. She's

discovered ways to produce her

pieces in great enough volume

to satisfy her market, and she's

found that good manners

smooth the path through unfa-

miliar territories.

A ONE-DAY WORKSHOP ON FELTMAKING GAVE CRISPINA HER CREATIVE DIRECTION. "In art school we had a one-day workshop on how to make handmade felt. As I was playing around with it, it just lent itself to these little stuffed toys I called Ragamuffins. There was a cooperative craft store in Cambridge, Massachusetts, where I first started selling my products. It comprised a wide range of people, from those who'd been highly trained to those who were just self-taught. They were my first inspiration and mentors.

"That first year all the Ragamuffins were made out of handmade felt, and they sold really well. My dad gave me the idea to use sweaters that had shrunk. Then I just started buying sweaters at thrift stores. I came up with a process that shrinks the knits to a feltlike texture but also leaves them soft.

"I turned this into a real business in 1987, when I was twenty-one, and since then it's just evolved. We (I have two assistants and a community of contract workers) actually take clothes, cut them up, and make them into blankets, rugs, and pillows. Now we're working on a project with American Apparel in Los Angeles, using their scrap for squares for our blankets. Why throw it in the Dumpster when we could be using it?

"THE ONLY BUSINESS EXPERIENCE I EVER HAD WAS WAITING TABLES, which sounds kind of crazy and almost like a cliché," adds Crispina, "but it was very valuable experience. In high school and college, I worked in a four-star, formal dining hotel, where I learned the code of manners,

BRIGHT
+ shirts

"If you have a skill and want to make a business from it, just go with that skill, push it past the limits and make it your own."

how to treat people, and always to be polite no matter what is said to you. That's actually very helpful for the business world."

YOU'LL FIND AN UNANTICIPATED SOURCE OF INSPIRATION COMES FROM BUSINESS SUCCESS ITSELF. "If somebody tells me they want to buy a thousand scarves—as a big company just did—that's inspiring to me because they obviously have found something about the product they like. I make my rugs like giant potholders,

and it works to use material that would otherwise have been trashed. I love it that people want to give me money for things like this, and I love making them."

Crispina credits her love for her craft and the joy she feels when exploring its potential with providing a solid base for her business. "If you have a skill and want to make a business from it, just go with that skill, push it past the limits, and make it your own. If you knit or crotchet or have a craft, make it yours, not what everybody else is doing. Second, I'd say listen and pay attention to what's out there in the market and what you can learn from other people—not so much formal training but everyday life. And be prepared to work hard."

❊ **HER DREAM** "The church is 12,000 square feet, 6,000 per floor, and has a twelve-bedroom rectory next door. It's incredibly cool. My husband and I want to create a community-oriented green design center with a restaurant. Honestly, my dream is to have time to garden, take care of babies, and influence the building of a culture with a slower pace. I think that would have to come from a different business model, one based on time, maybe, rather than production capacity."

---

* Marilyn Lysohir

COWGIRL CHOCOLATES

Moscow, Idaho

As Cowgirl Chocolates "head cowgirl" Marilyn Lysohir, ceramic sculptor turned specialty-sweets manufacturer, lives every child's dream: eating chocolate every day (for quality-control purposes only, of course). The transition isn't as strange as it seems; her very first job was in a chocolate factory. Years later, when her brother entered a contest and his idea of combining chocolate and hot pepper was mocked, Marilyn decided to prove him right and adapted his idea into a winning product. When a segment about the company aired on a national TV show and she got so much business that the Internet in Moscow, Idaho, crashed, she realized she was well on her way to thriving in dual careers.

✳ TRADE SECRETS

Marilyn Lysohir approaches her specialty chocolate business in much the same way she approaches her huge ceramic sculptures: cautiously, with each step planned. As a result, she balances art and business with apparent ease and understands that recognizing when to let go rather than pursue a project is bravery not failure.

"MY VERY FIRST JOB, WHEN I WAS SIXTEEN, WAS IN DAFFIN'S CHOCOLATE FACTORY in Sharon, Pennsylvania, and I worked there all the way through college. The owner, Pete Daffin, loved art, and he asked me if I'd do a four-foot chocolate bunny for the store for Easter. I said sure, but I got carried away and made it eight feet tall! He nearly fainted. We just barely got it in the door, and it caused a sensation. The customers loved it, especially the little kids. Chocolate morphed into art because I ended up making giant sculptures just like the bunny. Then, in 1995, my brother saw a contest offering $10,000 for a new chocolate flavor. He's an innocent person, and he thought, 'Oh, I'll just think of a flavor, and I'll get $10,000.' He wondered what would happen if you combined chocolate with hot pepper.

"He took his idea down to the company, but the staff made a big joke of it and laughed at him. That made me mad; I don't like mean-spiritedness. So I started experimenting with chocolate and cayenne pepper. You know how cowboy coffee is supposed to be so strong? Well, one person tried my chocolate and said, 'Whoa, these are cowboy chocolates!' I thought, 'There you go—Cowgirl Chocolates!'

"The Food Network contacted us in 2002, and *Unwrapped* filmed a segment. In July, they called and said, 'OK, now we're going to broadcast it.' My husband and I watched it and thought they did a really nice job and just went to bed. When the Internet system in Moscow, Idaho, went down that night, I knew this was something. We had a thousand orders: it was July—off-season for chocolate!

"**LIFE GIVES YOU CLUES.** I have to say that the way I run Cowgirl Chocolates is the same way that I think about art. It is a totally different animal, but there is a similarity of energy, thought, and inspiration with both art and the business. Be open and

"Your success is measured by your confidence, by your dependability, by your intellectual curiosity, and by your bravery."

it until I had my savings set up and I thought, 'Yeah, it is the right time; I'll try it.' It's not easy. It wasn't easy for me. Hopefully, women will use their creative spirits and just do great things. Know when to move and when not to, and know when to give up and try something else. That's not failure. Your success is measured by your confidence, by your dependability, by your intellectual curiosity, and by your bravery."

watch for the clues that come drifting by. If you ignore them, they just disappear, but if you can just be in the moment, you won't miss as many."

Despite the remarkable success that finds Marilyn overseeing a manufacturing facility with an on-site retail shop and a Web site for both retail and wholesale customers, she advocates: "Go slow. I want to understand where each step I take is leading. I'm cautious, so it takes longer. I paid my way through school, and it's the same thing with the business. I didn't start

✳ HER DREAM "I would like to sell the business and set up a trust fund for my brother. I'd do art or help whoever buys the business. I'm the head cowgirl; if they need me, I'm here to help."

Lori Mitchell ✳

LA DEE DAH FOLK ART

Richmond, Virginia

A twist of fate drove Lori Mitchell first to create her charmingly singular papier-mâché critters and then to work through various ways of marketing them. When a fledgling career as an animator was cut short by the sudden death of her mother, Lori returned home to help her dad care for her grandmother. Needing something she could do at home to support herself, she took the advice of a folk-artist

friend to try papier-mâché, and in a few short years, brought to life an entire world of whimsical creatures. She now sells the original figures directly to the public and also licenses them to a company that handles reproduction, marketing, and distribution to gift shops all over the country.

"I HAVE TO SAY THAT THE PEOPLE IN MY INDUSTRY ARE WONDERFUL. They gave me a lot of information and help," says Lori, when asked how her business came about. "My friend Jody Battaglia encouraged me to try papier-mâché, and I made one or two, maybe three, pieces. I actually learned the technique of papier-mâché in college. Through Jody, I met Debbee Thibault, also a successful folk artist, and when she saw my work she gave me the name and number of the rep who started her on her way. He had a special niche and his own private showroom, so that was a good beginning.

"I left the rep after a year and kept a few retail stores as customers. By the second year, the stores had created some buzz and other artists were finding out about me. People in the industry started collecting my work and saying 'Why don't you do this show, why don't you do that show?'"

A GROUP AD BROUGHT UNEXPECTED RESPONSE. "The promoter for a Christmas show I did on the West Coast wanted to take out a full-page ad in *Mary Englebreit's Home Companion* but needed help footing the bill. He asked nine artists to help out. In return we each had one piece photographed and our contact information included next to the picture. I would have had a hard time paying for coverage like that by myself. I had tons of people visit my Web site or e-mail me and sign up on my mailing list. It got my name out there and helped boost the sales of both my original works and my reproductions."

"If an opportunity was there, I had to try it."

Lori credits her early training and family for keeping her grounded and supporting her business. "My high-school homeroom teacher saw my drawings and advised me to get into art. He entered me in competitions; he really helped build my confidence and I got into art school. Starting this busi-

ness was a little bit of a necessity, but my dad and grandmother were so proud of me and that was very motivating.

Her father and grandmother have since passed away, and Lori is now married. "Any time obstacles would jump up, I was determined to solve them." She adds, "My husband's been in medical school for six years and that was a big driving force for me. Because of that, decisions that might have been difficult for somebody else were ones I just felt I had to make. If an opportunity was there, I had to try it."

Asked where the ideas for her quirky critters come from, Lori says, "I get inspiration from other folk artists, children's books, movies, and from colors and fabric. I think part of it is something about days gone by. But it comes from somewhere inside of me. I don't know where, but I've learned to trust myself." And as inspiration to other entrepreneurial artists, she adds: "My advice is to make what you would buy. That's huge."

✳ HER DREAM "Starting a family! I also want to spend some time taking my original sculptures to a grander level, with more involved and intricate one-of-a-kind designs."

---

*Lisa Norris

MADE BY ONE GIRL

Chattanooga, Tennessee

After leaving the South to attend art school in New York City, Lisa Norris found herself admiring sketchbooks she couldn't afford in the windows of stores, so she started making her own—the genesis of her flourishing whole-sale line of handmade blank books. "I wanted to figure out how I could make a living making art," she says. "I needed space, and there wasn't affordable space for me in New York. So I decided, 'I'm just going to go home.'" Now her career has two dimensions: The gracefully collaged fine-art dress-pattern pieces she affectionately calls "my girls" hang in museums and private collections, and her handmade books have turned up in Oscar bash gift bags.

"I DECIDED TO BUY A GIFT SHOP WITH MY DAD BECAUSE I THOUGHT I COULD LEARN SOME BUSINESS SKILLS and market my hand-made things and see if people would really pay for handmade photo albums," Lisa says of her endeavors on returning to Chattanooga. "I found out about juried art festivals and started entering them. Then some small shop owners asked if I wholesaled my stuff. At first I thought, 'No, I don't see how I can.' I had already streamlined my books a little for the general public.

All the while she was making her albums, Lisa was also creating her unusual fine-art collages. "The turning point came when the museum director here in town saw my dress-pattern collages. She really liked them and approached me about giving me a one-woman show at the museum. I thought, 'This is my sign.' I closed the gift shop and got a part-time job. I set aside certain hours to work in the studio. I didn't care if I was just sitting there drawing in my sketchbook. That really helped get the ball rolling."

Her business evolved along both lines. "With the books, I found I was taking too much time on each piece, so I toned them down a bit more—although they're still one-of-a-kind special—and now I can wholesale them. I exhibit my artwork at juried shows all over the Southeast and Midwest now. Sometimes I can exhibit books and artwork at the same show, but most of the time the show jury separates fine art and fine craft, and I do both.

"Some friends of mine who had a greeting-card company convinced me to do the stationery show in New York City, which I hadn't known about.

"I called all my buddies and said, 'I'll buy the beer and pizza. Come help me rip paper!'"

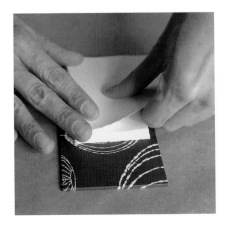

They said, 'This is where we get all our customers. Your books are good enough; you should give it a shot.' When I exhibited there in 2003, I got a huge response. Anthropologie called and wanted 150 books. I thought, 'Oh my god!' I got on the phone and called all my buddies and said, 'I'll buy the beer and pizza. Come help me rip paper!' And they did.

"PEOPLE ASK ME, 'HOW ARE YOU SO DISCIPLINED?' I DON'T EVEN THINK ABOUT IT ANYMORE. It's a way of life. It's how I operate. You have to make creativity a habit. It's like cooking or playing the piano: If you do it a lot, if you get into the habit, you are going to enjoy it more and more."

Lisa feels commitment—emotional and pragmatic—is crucial to dealing successfully with the unknown: "Be passionate about what you do and be quality oriented. Listen to what people have to say before you jump. Be strong in your convictions—know you can make it happen.

"I have a page in my sketchbook, and when I'm feeling all scared and think this is not going to work, I write down all the good things that have happened. It's been important for me to do that—it gets me back on the confidence trail."

✳ **HER DREAM** "To travel more and to have a retail venue for art and found objects. To have a place to teach workshops, with studio space. To have a place for art events of all kinds."

Barbara Schriber *

BARBARA SCHRIBER DESIGNS

Sandpoint, Idaho

The enthusiasm Barbara Schriber radiates is even brighter than the German glass glitter adorning her wholesale line of nostalgically appealing cards, papers, and hand-fashioned gift items. Unlike her mom, master crafter Melissa Neufeld, Barb saw herself as a linear-thinking, problem-solving management type with a future in finance. That is until her honeymoon, when husband Scott sug-

gested a detour to the small rural resort town of Sandpoint, which was so charming they decided to stay. Scott quickly found work as a carpenter, but Barb fretted she'd never find a job in her field. "Why don't you take this opportunity to figure out what you really want to do?" he suggested, and then packages of art supplies began arriving from her mother.

Just arrived

Le premier baiser.

Toast à la prospérité des mariés

"I NEVER BELIEVED I HAD AN OUNCE OF CREATIVITY IN ME," insists Barbara, whose line includes winsome cards that are based on her collection of circa-1800 postcards and spectacular crowns for celebrating almost any occasion. "My mom is an amazing designer, but I thought her genes had skipped me! When Scott encouraged me not to rush into a job, she sent me tools and materials and tons of support. She'd send me clippings from magazines to point out techniques and design ideas and told me, 'Just start something and see where it takes you.' She gave me my first opportunity, finishing a job for a client of hers, and that turned into a few others. I put together a very crude catalog and mailed it to stores I knew or had read about, and Barbara Schriber Designs was born. I think so many people have creative abilities and don't even know it; all they need to discover their talent is the opportunity to try.

About her career transition, Barbara says "The biggest change I made was one of character: I learned that failure is not the worst thing in the world and that fear of it was my biggest obstacle. Once I accepted that failure was an option, it actually freed me to take my mother's advice and believe that every first step can lead to something fabulous, even if it's the result of many mistakes, especially if it's the result of many mistakes."

HOW YOU WORK CAN BE VITAL. "Someone will say 'Can you come up with something for a bridal shower?' and that will give me a task. I have a hard time working in a vacuum, without guidelines.

✳ TRADE SECRETS

Barbara Schriber is living proof that taking time to nurture creativity can have amazing results: Her charming paper goods are found in specialty shops nationwide. She's realized that facing failure as a possibility is liberating and understands that how a business is organized may be as important as what is produced. The heart of it all, she believes, is remaining true to your beliefs.

"Part of using professionals is recognizing your weaknesses so you can get help in those areas."

Also, my mom taught me that if everything isn't in plain sight and readily accessible, you won't think to use it. My workspace has four workstations with deep countertops; each station has drawers full of their own tools.

CHOOSE THE SCOPE UP FRONT, BARBARA URGES. "Determine in the beginning if you want to just design or do you want to run a business; they're two paths, each with pros and cons. I love the business part but it does take away from designing. If you want to just design, I think licensing your work and getting an agent is best. If you want to do both, I'd advise bringing in professionals to do the business end, which is hard in the beginning because of the money. Part of using professionals is recognizing your weaknesses so you can get help in those areas.

"I learned so much from helping with my mother's business when I was young, communicating with sales reps, learning about licensing and order management. Without it I would have had a longer learning curve. I sell wholesale because I saw how retail and wholesale businesses work and I think wholesale is better. If you have a small company and design cards and crowns and sell to the general public, you'd sell one card here and one crown there—you have to process it, package it, ship it, invoice it. That's time that's so hard to account for, but a big wholesale order uses that time so much more efficiently; expanding and contracting with the economy is much easier."

✳ **HER DREAM** "There aren't many jobs in this town, and I want to have a company that provides a good one with benefits for single mothers. Women need to help women. I've had all sorts of people tell me I'll go out of business because I refuse to go overseas for manufacturing. That may be true, but I'm trying to help my local economy. My dream has always been to build a life I'm happy with."

✳ Jane Zaccaria

TIDDLYWINKS & SCALLYWAGS

Glen Ellyn, Illinois

Jane Zaccaria is now a successful designer of a wholesale line of little girls' clothing, but her path has not been a straightforward one. Growing up in Britain, Jane learned to knit, crochet, and sew. Her dad made patterns for clothes for Cindy, the British Barbie, and her mother was an award-winning knitter. By the time she was eight Jane knew she wanted to be a designer. But the economic picture in Britain at the end of the 1980s was dim, so when she went off to college it was to develop her math skills in pursuit of a steady paycheck. Years later, married with two sons and living in the United States, she gave birth to a daughter. When she began to look for clothing for her little girl, Jane *knew* she could do better.

JANE REALIZED THERE WAS A MARKET WAITING WHEN THE AGE-APPROPRIATE CLOTHES SHE MADE FOR HER DAUGHTER attracted the attention of other parents. "The clothes available for little girls were great until my daughter turned three. Then the styles, in my opinion, jumped from little girl to big girl, so I started making clothes for her. As I became more and more creative, people started noticing that my child was dressed differently and inquired where I got the clothes. So that is really how the business came about, making things for my own daughter and then for a few friends and then turning that into sort of a home-based business of designing and actually constructing garments a couple of times a year."

A whimsical twist of fate gave her early endeavors a boost, Jane explains. "My daughter was in a dance recital, and she had a real stiff tutu. At the end of the performance, she said to me from the stage, 'Mommy is it over now?' She promptly pulled the tutu down in front of the audience! She is really a character, my daughter. That gave me the idea for the tutus. She is totally my inspiration.

"I started selling tutus and pillows made of vintage fabrics at bazaars featuring artists with really good-quality crafts, and I sold out. I made twenty-two tutus and they sold in one hour. That was the pivotal 'lightbulb moment' when I said, 'Oooh, I think I can make a living doing this!'

"FINDING A MANUFACTURER BECAME A NECESSITY," Jane recognized at that point. "I just don't enjoy making forty of the same thing. I had

"I made twenty-two tutus, and they sold in one hour. That was the pivotal 'lightbulb moment.'"

already been buying the component parts—the tulle, ribbon, elastic. Then I opened my retail shop. I had contacts, and those people put me in touch with other people. It's all about networking."

Purveying quality children's clothing at a profitable price presents some challenges. "One of the biggest obstacles, I suppose, has been getting the customer to understand that there is a difference between homemade and handmade. You know, *art* is handmade. It's about a level of skill, design, and quality where crafts are put together so perfectly. It's not just having a hot-glue gun and making masses of stuff. Getting the customer to understand that has been crucial."

As the business grew, Jane continues, "I closed my retail shop to concentrate on my goal of marketing my products to a wider audience. I now attend shows to market my goods to boutiques in the demographics I've learned my clothing style fits best: the sunny states of California and Florida and the South."

✳ **HER DREAM** "To actually have a brand rather than a specific product. And to live by the ocean!"

Amie Sikes, *
Jolie Sikes-Smith,
& Janie Sikes

THE JUNK GYPSY COMPANY

College Station, Texas

The Junk Gypsies (Amie, left, sister Jolie, right, and mom Janie, center) whose blazingly fast-growing retail apparel and accessories line has gained them brand status, are much more than a business; they're a way of life. When Amie took her first job in the corporate world and ended up sitting in endless traffic with runs in her stockings, she said, "Forget it," and headed home, where she

and Janie took $2,000 and hit the flea-market and antiques show circuit buying and selling funky old furniture. It wasn't long before Jolie joined them. When they put their slogan "Well Behaved Women Rarely Make History" on a T-shirt, their suspicions were confirmed—inside every woman beats a junk-loving, gypsy heart—and their apparel line was born.

"WE STARTED BACKWARD FROM THE WAY MOST PEOPLE BUILD A BUSINESS." Janie and husband Philip always had their own businesses, running several restaurants, and Amie and Jolie grew up helping out. Both sisters had vague professional plans, but that entrepreneurial itch was in their genes, and it flourished on the flea-market circuit, where their booths turned into parties that got so big they became "events," like their twice-yearly Junk-O-Rama Prom. Jolie says, "We didn't start with a store like most people do. We built it more like a musician would, from the grassroots level, like we were on tour traveling to different places, meeting different people, making friends. Our customers feel like they had a part in it all. We didn't know it, but we were in the early stages of building a brand."

AMIE: "We weren't selling just one thing. We were selling furniture and all kinds of funky stuff, a mix of new and old, a whole lot of different looks combined; that's what began our Junk Gypsy style. We're inspired by everything from the Suffragettes to Jesse James of West Coast Choppers and by lots of music.

"Starting our own clothing line was an accident. We'd been using the quote 'Well behaved women rarely make history.' So we put it on a shirt with these miniature cowgirls from this old picture we had, and we thought it'd be fun."

JOLIE: "Like a souvenir T-shirt."

JANIE: "When we got the shirts unloaded at the first show, we couldn't even get them out before the women saw them and started digging

✳ TRADE SECRETS

Almost intuitively the Junk Gypsies have turned their sassy fun-to-the-end flair into a brand. They've remained true to their quirky ethos, carefully and constantly editing their products, knowing that it's their vision that builds customer loyalty. They're not afraid of success and understand that saying no to opportunities can be just as important as saying yes.

"If you want to start your own business, don't copy everybody else. You can really sell it better if it comes from what you believe in."

into the boxes! That was a pretty good indication to us we needed to go further with this."

JOLIE: "We're starting to manufacture them . . ."

AMIE: ". . . from the ground up, where we decide every stitch, not just the art that's on them."

STRONG AND VARIED PARTNERSHIPS GIVE STRENGTH TO A NEW BUSINESS, Amie explains: "We've formed alliances with a lot of different people because we sell a lot not just at flea markets but through our Web site, and we're also in cahoots with a couple of country musicians, Miranda Lambert and Dierks Bentley. Some of our strongest alliances are with the music world: They help us by wearing our stuff and having our name on their products because we do a lot of their design work and we promote them to our customers. It's a great collaboration. They're big artists, but we help a lot of local musicians, too. We have a pretty good customer base, and we can promise local musicians a big turnout at our events and we pay them well!"

JOLIE: "Like at the Junk-O-Rama Prom we just had, there were 1,200 people, and we had three different musicians play at that."

AMIE: "If you want to start your own business, don't copy everybody else. You can really sell it better if it comes from what you believe in. We never quit reading and researching—*Fortune* and *Inc.* magazines—and we want to stay true to who we are and what this business is all about. If you just want to make money, you're going to be let down pretty quickly. It's very important to listen to your customers, but at the same time if you only sell what you think they want you to sell. . ."

JOLIE: ". . . you're selling out. If something isn't our style, we're not going to sell it. We want to stay true to what the business is all about."

PROVIDING AN EXPERIENCE IS KEY. The Junk Gypsies offer more than just an everyday shopping experience. Their attitude and aesthetic infuse their market booth and Web site, offering fun and flamboyance to everyone who visits. Janie remarks: "An article about us said the Junk Gypsies don't have customers, they have fans. We have women drive across the country just to come to Prom and see us!"

✳ **THEIR DREAM** JOLIE: "We feel we're not just a retail industry; we also have some sort of social responsibility to do the right thing. We've been approached by a lot of groups and we're being careful. We're going to go ahead and put in a number of stores, starting in Austin, and do a catalog business, and we have plans for our online Wild Blue Yonder Fund for activities we believe in. Our dream all along has been just to be happy with what we do."

JANIE: "To all work together."

AMIE: "A lot of people are just working 'til they get to retirement so they can do what they really want. That's not us. We're doing what we want right now; this business is our dream."

---

* Judy Godwin

CLASSIC CATERING

Camden, Maine

A serial remodeler not only of houses but also of herself, Judy Godwin has gone from salesperson to retail antiques dealer to caterer. When she became a mother at forty-two, she was a high-powered salesperson but didn't want to delegate raising her child. Luckily, her employer, a women's health consulting firm, let her bring her daughter to work, but when the one-year-old began crawling into the bosses' offices, it was time to go. So she took her love of old houses and her collection of antiques, moved to Maine, and opened her antiques and interiors business, specializing in large architectural pieces. Later, after being sidelined by a nearly fatal accident, Judy retreated to the heart of her home, her kitchen, and began cooking up a new life.

"Everything should be in writing, with all the details spelled out. That protects the client and the caterer."

✳ TRADE SECRETS

Judy Godwin's ability to self-invent informs her business decisions. After closing her antiques business she turned to her first love, cooking, and now uses her collections of antique linens and tableware to bring unparalleled elegance to her catering business. While an advocate of following your heart, she knows that being well organized and on top of every detail is the cornerstone of a successful endeavor.

RECOGNIZING THE POTENTIAL OF HER AVO-CATIONS helped Judy to change her career more than once. "I watched Oprah for years. She kept talking about that 'lightbulb moment,' and I thought, 'Oh please, let me find the thing that feeds my soul.' And then I realized that I had been doing it since I was twenty-five! I love remodeling houses, and I had collected tons of antiques over the years, so I became an antiques dealer.

"I could take my daughter to school, do my booth in a group shop, and still have time to be involved in her school and other activities. And that led me here, because Maine is antiques Mecca.

"After my accident, I said, 'Now I have to do something easy; I'll be a caterer!' What a joke; catering is the hardest work I've ever done, but it's also the most rewarding. I use all the antiques I have collected all these years—all the linens and china and baskets and serving pieces—so my catering is about a beautifully styled event, as well as, I hope, wonderful food."

GOOD SPACE, GOOD PLACE, AND GOOD PLANNING is Judy's recipe for success. "I always have a good kitchen. I love to cook, and the kitchen is the heart of the home. I bought a ten-foot-long and ten-foot-tall French hardware cabinet. I told the woman I bought it from, 'Don't ever sell me anything again unless my therapist is with me!' I had no place to put it, but I loved it, so I built a house around it, and it's my pantry!

"I cooked dinner for four yesterday and got everything from my herb garden. I used nasturtiums. I barely knew what they were until I came to Maine! I decorated my risotto torte with a sprig of rosemary from my herb garden. For me, being able to walk out my kitchen door and cut herbs in this beautiful environment is heaven. That's what I'm about. That's my inspiration."

But the business of creating perfect dinner parties requires meticulous organization, too: "I write down everything. I schedule, outline, and plan. I'm very organized, and yet I still make checklists because I can't afford to miss one little thing. I bring all the linens, silver, glassware, and serving pieces, which requires many lists. For catering, everything should be in writing with all the details spelled out. That protects the client and the caterer.

"You absolutely have to do what you love in life. My mother told me not to do that, and that's why I began so late. I should have been doing this at twenty!"

✳ **HER DREAM** "I've wanted my own restaurant my whole life, and not a chain, just enough room for ten guests. It needs to be small to be right for me. And I would really love my daughter to work with me."

✳ Marcia Gottlieb, ASID

MARCIA GOTTLIEB INTERIORS

Winston-Salem, North Carolina

When she started her interior design business, boats launched and ladies lunched, but Marcia Gottlieb's gracious professionalism and classic look built a career that has spanned four decades. Finding that women were held to higher standards, particularly in the early days of her business, Marcia set out to master both her field and the complexities of running a business. Now on her second generation of clients, with more schedule problems than ever—her female clients have demanding jobs of their own these days—Marcia is at that golden moment of enjoying all she's achieved.

"I think word of mouth, particularly in a small community, is so important."

✳ TRADE SECRETS

Marcia Gottlieb has never

wavered in her conviction that

women in business must

adhere to the highest standards

of professionalism. She keeps

her interior-design eye honed,

following trends across a

spectrum of sources, and

attends as diligently to routine

tasks as to creative ones. Word

of mouth, she feels, may be the

best publicity of all.

A CAREER LIKE INTERIOR DESIGN CAN EVOLVE OVER TIME: You can work for others or for yourself as suits your needs. Marcia started by "doing design work for friends and was approached by a beautiful furniture store to work part time. I had two children at that point and was a better mother for working. Ten years later, when a friend started his own business, I joined him. The American Society of Interior Design [ASID] was just forming, so we organized a study group to prepare for the National Council for Interior Design Qualification [NCIDQ] exam, and I took some courses at the local college. I passed that exam on pure determination! In 1991 my partner wanted to retire, so I started my own firm. I thought I'd slow down, but I was busier than ever; even a bout with cancer didn't slow me down much."

KEEPING YOUR EYES OPEN AND EDUCATED IS CRITICAL IN ANY DESIGN FIELD; doing so provides the inspiration and resources that lead ultimately to satisfied clients and a good reputation. Marcia remarks, "Magazines are a great part of my inspiration, not just the design and shelter magazines but fashion magazines like *Vogue* or *Bazaar*. I think one thing follows the other. Color also inspires me. I don't do very trendy interiors, but I certainly must know what's happening in all the creative fields.

"Winston-Salem is a wonderful area for fine crafts, and I encourage my clients to use them. In a very traditional setting, I will use contemporary art. Art makes a room personal, so I suggest that

my clients visit galleries and just look. I go with them; I love that.

"I've had press coverage through the years and participated in show houses, and magazines like *House Beautiful* have covered them. But I think word of mouth, particularly in a small community—people seeing your work in the home of the president of a bank and so forth—is so important. I think that as a woman you need to be more professional than any man. Perhaps that's true in every field. I've done that, and people are willing to pay for my expertise."

"PROBABLY 40 PERCENT OF WHAT I DO IS CREATIVE, AND 60 PERCENT IS LEGWORK: writing purchase orders, writing the orders to my workroom on how to make draperies. If the draperies are two inches too short, for example, that's my profit—gone. But I have to fix it. Is there enough fabric? Is it from the same dye lot? All those details. That's also the difference between having a successful business or not—the bottom line.

"Of necessity I've built numerous relationships. I am dependent on so many people: the person making the

know more than interior designers."

Marcia advises anyone interested in an interior-design career to "work on the sales floor of a nice furniture store or fabric showroom to see what it's all about. You should get as much schooling as you can. I personally would not go to design school without going to college first. I feel very strongly about that. Breadth of experience helps, but many successful designers have had very little schooling. They got jobs at design firms; that's wonderful training. The truth is, overnight success is rare in this field."

She offers guidance for keeping the professional and personal separate. "You have to clearly define the difference between friendships and professional relationships. You have to be careful because a friend may think you can get her a sofa at a cheap price or, sofa, the salesperson selling me the fabric, painters, installers, brick layers. And it's terribly important to have good relationships with architects because some wrongly think they because working on someone's home is so intense, you become friends with clients. I'm very diligent about what role I'm playing. I'll say, 'I'm putting on my professional hat now.'"

✳ **HER DREAM** "To limit my practice, but I haven't quite figured out how to do that yet! I have three children and seven grandchildren with whom I want to spend more time. I'm at a new place for me."

Marki McMillan *
& Rae Lynn White

FRANCISKA'S HOUSE

La Grange, Texas

On five private acres at the top of a hill outside of Houston rests an oasis of tranquillity, a bed-and-breakfast named Franciska's House. A labor of love by two former antiques dealers, Marki McMillan (left) and partner Rae Lynn White, it brings serenity to its visitors and has empowered Marki and Rae Lynn to pursue dreams they hadn't believed possible. Since opening Franciska's House, they've both embarked on new careers and at the same time are looking into operating a second, larger, bed-and-breakfast.

"WE KNEW WE WANTED TO DO A B AND B BUT WE DIDN'T KNOW WHERE, HOW, OR WHEN," explains Rae Lynn. "I'd heard that if you can visualize something, you can make it happen. We got a little binder and pulled out pictures from magazines. We slipped them into plastic protectors and labeled the binder 'Country House Dream Book,' I kid you not! And then the house appeared. It was the most magical thing.

"The first time we saw the house, in 1998, the whole way back to Houston we were brainstorming. We stopped at a Pizza Hut and sat there with a pad of paper just running through all the possibilities: How can we afford it and how can we make it work from a distance? That's the part that boggled us. It had to be unhosted because we live an hour and a half away in Houston.

MARKI ELABORATES: "It's a dream many people have, to have one life in the city and another in the country. I think it was the creative outlet we were both looking for. I had some background in event planning and operations management, and I'd done some catering."

RAE LYNN ADDS: "And I've always been in sales and marketing. That was pretty much the division of labor going into this. By chance I was in an easy job at that time, so I had the emotional and mental energy to put the house together. Everyday while I was working I was making lists of what we needed to do, then running to Home Depot to pick up things. We dragged everything from Houston. We just worked, worked, worked for six months."

✳ **TRADE SECRETS**

With no staff on-site, Marki McMillan and Rae Lynn White's unhosted B and B is truly unique. The very best products and furnishings maintain the magic so that guests fall in love with the experience; repeat business drives the venture. Success, the partners have realized, is empowering!

"If you can visualize
something you can
make it happen."

MARKI COUNTERS: "I didn't have
that kind of freedom. Rae Lynn was
definitely the organizer, the one with
the flow chart."

RAE LYNN: "Well, she's exagger-
ating. I had my yellow legal pad and
list, but I was more exhausted than I
have ever been in my life. It took six
months from purchase to opening.
Then, during the big antiques show in
Round Top [Texas], we had a huge
party and introduced it to people."

THEY FELT THE TARGET MARKET
WAS PEOPLE LIKE THEM, MARKI
EXPLAINS. "We asked ourselves what
we would want if we walked into a
place away from the stresses and
strains of daily life with no one else
around? That's what makes it different. The space itself is magical. We
were given that gift to work with, we
just enhanced it with all the special
touches you don't give yourself at
home. We paid a lot of attention
to details like fabrics, color, and textures, from luxurious bed linens
down to really nice soaps and wonderful things in the bathroom. The
house is filled with antiques and cot-
tage-style upholstered furniture and
fresh-cut flowers, many from native
plants grown right there. When you
open the refrigerator, there's homemade quiche and fresh fruit juice. We
drive out before guests arrive, set
everything up and then disappear.
You get to peek into another world,
and it's all yours."

RAE LYNN CONTINUES: "People
have a love affair with the house and
keep coming back; it's like their
second home. They send us gifts for
the house like drawer sachets or do
paintings of the wild flowers or leave
notes about the gourmet dinner they

fixed and how they sat under the stars and saw a meteor shower."

SERENDIPITY GOT THEM OFF TO A GOOD START. Rae Lynn says, "I hate the word *networking*, but a friend of Marki's mother who's an antiques dealer came to our introductory party and she turned out to be friends with an editor of *Country Living*, and they did a story."

And success revealed new possibilities for both women. Marki says, "The surprising thing was that because we did this so well and it was such a success, we realized that we actually could do things we'd wanted to do for a long time. I had wanted to go to graduate school, and Rae Lynn had wanted to get into real estate, so that's what we're doing now. Franciska's House hasn't freed us financially, but it has enabled us to envision doing what we've wanted to do. *Empowering* is the best word."

Rae Lynn: "It enabled us to fly. I felt we had wings. Once you have a success like this, you understand you can make anything happen. My favorite quote, from Goethe, says, 'Whatever you can do or dream you can do, begin it. Boldness has genius, power, and magic in it. Begin it now.'"

✳ **THEIR DREAM** MARKI: "We're in the planning stages of acquiring another fabulous place with three houses. We'll run that from Houston, too, but there will be somebody on-site, because it's a bigger property. Maybe we'll venture into marketing it as a place for conferences or retreats."

RAE LYNN: "We already bought three rugs for it!"

Lucinda Rooney *

LUCINDA ROONEY, LLC

Middlebury, Vermont

Lucinda Rooney presides over an incredibly gorgeous garden and offers her services for floral and garden design, teaches at prestigious institutions, and appears on television. Raised by her grandparents on a small farm in the Adirondack Mountains, she spent hours in her grandmother's garden. From there it was off to study horticulture at a college in Vermont and then at the renowned Royal Botanic Garden in Kew, England. Yet in the brief time span of a few years she dealt with an array of some of life's most distressing events, handling them all with a combination of boundless charm and enthusiasm and the steely determination common to all true entrepreneurs.

"I like the word *relationships* better than *networking* because people in this world are interconnected."

AN ENVIABLE QUOTIENT OF SELF-CONFIDENCE
ENABLED LUCINDA TO MOVE FROM STUDENT
TO PRO IN SHORT ORDER. She explains, "While
at the Royal Botanic Garden I was able to go to
the Chelsea Flower Show and see fantastic floral
arrangements that were spectacular yet so natural.
Inspired by the show, I came home and opened my
business. I put $5,000 on my credit card to get
brochures and business cards made up to portray
the person I knew I could become in this industry.
I strongly believed I could create an excellent
product, but I hadn't really done it yet, so I used
the money to create the look.

"Soon afterward I became head gardener at
Shelburne Farms, here in Vermont, just as they
started doing weddings. I was able to show what I
could do right off the bat. That's when I knew I
was right."

That self-confidence has been nurtured since
childhood. She recalls: "When I got the lead in
The Wizard of Oz in eighth grade, my music
teacher said to me, 'Congratulations, Lucinda. I
just want you to know, you weren't the best, but
you sure were the loudest!' That's been my business motto since I was thirteen!"

Lucinda suggests successful custom design
requires an emotional connection. "Put yourself in
an environment that makes you feel creative.
Instead of trying to re-create Provence in your
backyard, figure out what it is exactly about
Provence that inspires you. Then you can create
that emotion in your own space. What I've always
done is saturate myself with places, experiences,

✳ TRADE SECRETS

Lucinda Rooney knows
firsthand that a deep-seated
belief in your own abilities
can justify risks that the more
fearful would shun. She
networks with those she
admires and makes the
personality of each customer
central to her floral and garden
designs. She embraces
serendipitous breaks but
learned a long time ago that
it's drive, not luck, that fuels
a successful career.

books, or environments that make me feel creative."

Lucinda is unique in her approach to design: "The way I design is more about the person, the customer, than the flowers. I use the flowers to interpret the customer's personality and who she or he is. Flowers have such diverse characters, so that when the designer is attuned to the customer and uses flowers as the medium, she can really represent people's personalities through them. Flowers have a wonderful way of conveying emotion."

COLLABORATION IS KEY. "I like the word *relationships* better than *networking* because people in this world are interconnected. You have something to give, and they have something you need; the collaboration strengthens the relationship. It's not one-sided or self-centered; it's about what you are giving, not getting. I've always thought you should network or associate with the people you want to become. Don't ever go below your standards."

Self-confidence is important, but Lucinda suggests that discretion is equally valuable. "Be very careful with whom you share your enthusiasm. Some friends won't like what you're doing because they would never take such risks. It's a projection of their own fear. I have learned to keep my big ideas to myself until I bring them to fruition. Then I share them."

✳ **HER DREAM** "The more my passion was shaped to my purpose the more I started living. I want to inspire women and men to follow *their* purpose, to let them know they can do it. My flowers are just the way I communicate this phenomenal life I have gotten to live."

---

* Kate Shifrin

COME FLEA WITH ME

Niles, Illinois

For years Kate Shifrin and sister Christie Weller—cofounders of their aptly named excursion business, Come Flea with Me— beat back attempts by friends to join them on their Saturday flea-market expeditions, claiming there wasn't room in the truck. When they realized it was down-right mean not to share the fun, they got a big comfy bus and began signing up an ever-expanding list of customers to hit the highways and byways looking for the best markets. Now they've taken to the skies as well, taking groups of intrepid shoppers to the fabled markets of Paris.

Kate Shrifin has cleverly taken the great idea of guided flea-market tours and parlayed it into the beginnings of an empire. She began with a cold-blooded assessment of the dedication needed to start a business and protected her venture by implementing professional financial and legal advice. Among other rewards, the discovery of her customers' enjoyment is exhilarating.

"I HAVE YEARS OF RETAIL EXPERIENCE, BUT I PROMISED MYSELF I'D HAVE MY OWN BUSINESS BY THE TIME I WAS THIRTY-FIVE. After I realized that taking people on old-fashioned field trips was what I wanted to do, I opened the checking account, got a credit card, got my office set up—and took a very deep breath and jumped. I'm also lucky that my husband has a financial and legal background. He's a great support and help to me. He told me, 'Get the name trademarked. It's a great name; it's a great idea. You have to protect yourself to the best of your ability.'"

Flea marketing was in Kate's blood. "When we were kids our parents would drive to Florida on vacation, and we'd stop at so many yard sales that by the time we got there our noses would almost be touching the roof of the car, there'd be so much stuff under us! Our backyard patio was covered in oriental rugs, and the planters were big pickle barrels cut in half."

About starting Come Flea with Me, she says, "I told myself, 'I've picked up some great skills along the way. You know what? I'm going to give it a try.'" She explains that once the deep breath is taken and the leap made, "It's really about the self-discipline of managing your day. It's being sensible and asking yourself the logical questions: Is this something people want? Am I passionate enough to hang in there? That's important because the phone may not ring on day one or day two, and until that phone starts ringing, you have to figure out how to market yourself and your business. Your workday is figuring out how to get that phone to

> "Starting a business is a business. It's not just coming up with a cute idea. Anything that succeeds takes a tremendous amount of work."

ring. Starting a business is a business. It's not coming up with a cute idea and sitting down in some little office. Anything that succeeds takes a tremendous amount of work.

"I THINK THE DESIRE TO DO IT WAS STRONGER THAN THE FEAR. I think lack of courage is the number-one obstacle. You have to believe in what you are doing and in your abilities. I think for a lot of people it's a big thing to admit 'I can handle this. I am worthy.'"

And happily for Kate, Come Flea with Me was worthy of good press. She says her big break was "Publicity. Pretty much right out of the gate we were in *Lucky* magazine and appeared twice in *Chicago* magazine. *Lucky* magazine, being a national magazine, was a huge deal. It exposed us to so many more people. It was an enormous reach out."

Kate sums it up: "I didn't realize how people would react, but the energy and inspiration and friendship we receive are intoxicating. People tell me they feel like they've been on vacation. At the end of a trip I think, 'Oh my goodness! Not only is it working, but they love it too!'"

✳ **HER DREAM** "To create an empire! We want to take people to flea markets across the country, but that's only fifty states, so we're going international. We'd also like a TV show walking people through flea markets around the world, exposing them to antiques and markets they may never have heard of."

Maurrie Sussman *

SISTERS ON THE FLY

Phoenix, Arizona

Maurrie Sussman's Sisters on the Fly invites women to throw off everyday cares (or lifelong worries) and, for fees ranging from $200 to $2,000, spend some time fly fishing under Montana's "big sky" or learning to ride, rope, and herd cattle at Cowgirl College in Wyoming—martini in hand. What started as just a small group of women having a great time exploded when Maurrie came up  with the idea of refurbishing vintage trailers, which she sells, and leading their owners on her adventures. For those who really get into life on the range there's the Cowgirl Caravan, a membership organizations of "sisters." To complement the trips, Maurrie has built a web of partnerships with vendors and venues and even has her own Western-themed bedding line.

"We get so much
media coverage
because I always
say 'yes.'"

COWGIRL COLLEGE, COWGIRL CARAVAN, AND THEMED BEDDING—HOW DID SHE COME UP WITH ALL THIS? For someone who started with a business degree, went into the hotel industry, then had an antiques shop and ran a catering business, what else would you end up doing?

Maurrie recounts, "As a child I wanted to be a bush pilot. In my day, though, women weren't allowed to do stuff like that. My dad said, 'Nope, girls aren't pilots.' But our mom took us camping and fishing and hiking, and we had the best time.

"My son grew up to be a fly-fisherman, and I'd go with him. My sister Becky and my mom, Maisie, eighty-six, would visit, and they loved it, too. One night Becky and I were floating down the Madison River drinking a glass of wine and watching the eagles, and we decided—because all of our friends were so jealous of the way we just get in our trucks and go across the country—to invite friends and that's how it started.

"I found a 1958 Holiday trailer; her name is Lucy. As soon as I looked at her, I fell madly in love. So I immediately brought her home and started decorating her. Then my sister saw her, and she got one. Then it just went nuts after that."

Marveling, Maurrie continues, "Sisters on the Fly has become so large, we're up to 650 sisters. (Since it started with sisters, everyone who joins becomes a sister, too.) We have the Cowgirl Caravans with the trailers, nearly all of which are decorated. We go fishing, horseback riding, or antiquing, drink wine, and talk about our trailers. We do adventures like Cowgirl College at a ranch.

※ TRADE SECRETS

For Maurrie Sussman, hosting nontradtional vacations for women started as a lark—and it still is! Turning her venture into a money-making operation, Maurrie found corporate partners and created ancillary products. Restoring a vintage trailer provided a compelling image that led to great media coverage and new recruits eager to join the community of Sisters on the Fly.

"When we first started talking about making money at this we got some of the big fishing gear companies to sponsor us. I make cowgirl bedding, too. Right here in my little office, I have a huge cutting table. When I'm very stressed trying to put these trips together, I come over and start cutting away at making quilts."

YES IS THE MAGIC WORD. "We get so much media coverage because I always say 'yes.' If anyone calls and asks us to please bring the trailers for an event, I always say 'yes,' and that's networking, because we're giving back to the community. You can always tell when we've been on TV because we get five new girls signing up."

Seeing satisfied "sisters" is tremendously rewarding. Maurrie says much of her own satisfaction comes from "watching the girls learn to love being outdoors, fishing or cowgirling on a horse. I had one girl sobbing, 'Please, Maurrie, don't make me get on this horse!' I said, 'You came all the way from Tennessee. You drove your trailer for the first time. You are here in Arizona at Cowgirl College. You're getting on that horse, and that's the way it's going to be!' She ended up having the best time. She won all the awards. Later she called me and said, 'This is Margie. I want you to know I just went to the store to return some lipstick and I came home with a yellow pickup to match my trailer.'"

Maurrie has these words of advice for would-be entrepreneurs: "Sit down with a piece of paper and a pencil, and write down everything you like and can do. It's as simple as that. Sit by yourself with a martini, maybe in a swimming pool, naked; it makes you open up. All these things surface: This is what I love, this is what inspires me, and this is what gives me courage."

✳ **HER DREAM** "We want to expand into new adventures, go kayaking in New Zealand. I want to take it to a different level, as far as it will go. We've built a real community. It's pretty amazing to watch the dynamics of the women. That's the fun part. I want to take women on adventures until I'm 103—and be a bush pilot."

Business-Crafting Workshop

The Business Plan

If you have even a glimmer of an entrepreneurial idea you should consider setting aside time to think seriously about your own dream business. Spending a weekend or a series of Saturday mornings working through the steps required to develop a business plan could be just what you need to realize "Yes! I *can* do this, I can live my dream!"

KNOW WHERE YOU'RE GOING

It's an old joke that men navigating unfamiliar roads drive their female companions wild by refusing to ask for directions. So capable, competent women who want to launch their own businesses shouldn't shy away from writing a business plan, which is simply a road map to a destination—in this case, an entrepreneurial creative life.

While passion is essential, you'll need to be specific if you want to reach your goal. Begin with an idea of what you want to do—an idea that's as clear as possible. As you develop the plan for making your dream real, be open to the potential of your business as well as its limitations, and refine it until you can articulate it and see it in three dimensions and full color: You want one of those touring maps with an icon for each attraction along the way.

DO YOUR HOMEWORK

Knowledge—or lack of it—can make the difference between the success and failure of a business. Cheryl A. Mills, associate deputy administrator of entrepreneurial development for the Small Business Administration (SBA), urges every potential entrepreneur to become educated about her dream business and the steps for making it happen. She stresses four key points to research:

THE MARKET: Learn about the market for your particular goods or services and then learn how to meet its needs.

THE BUSINESS OF YOUR BUSINESS: Learn how to put together a solid business plan and figure out how you'll manage the business itself.

THE MONEY: Calculate how much financing you'll need and research the options for putting it together.

EXPERT HELP: Luckily, there are numerous resources available to help you develop your plan; take advantage of them. Good places to start include the Small Business Administration (SBA), the Women's Business Center, and SCORE: Counselors to America's Small Business. There are many other sources that offer advice; find out what and where they are (see Resources on page 184 of this book to get started).

As you undertake your research, talk to your friends and contacts, get on the Internet, and go to the library. When you've learned as much as you can, it's time to move on to the actual plan.

CRAFT YOUR PLAN

All business plans cover basically the same principles (see Five Essentials of

---

✳ BUSINESS PLAN ✳ CHECKLIST

A business plan is a tool for determining the feasibility of your dream and guiding its growth. The process of developing the plan is straightforward.

- Define your business clearly so that you can accurately communicate your vision.

- Research the components of an effective business plan; learn all you can about your market; do realistic financial planning.

- Write the plan yourself; this is the best way to learn what you need to know to be true to your vision and well prepared to open your doors.

- Take advantage of consultants; you needn't (and probably won't be able to) figure it all out for yourself.

- Give it a professional format that reflects your commitment: Include a table of contents and an executive summary so an overview is readily accessible. Type it neatly and bind it.

Every Business Plan, page 151). The chapters that follow in this workshop provide an overview of the concepts

- **VICKI MOTE BODWELL,** *children's bedding designer:* My business plan—I do one every year—gives me data points. I check the projections in it against actual results, make adjustments, and have headed off problems as a result.

- **MARCIA GOTTLIEB,** *interior designer:* Time is a factor in building the relationships that make a business a success. You have to be patient.

- **AMIE SIKES,** *apparel and accessories retailer:* There's no secret to starting a business. It's do what you love and be willing to work your booty off. Some people say, "Oh, I just can't catch a break," but you make your own breaks, and things fall through all the time. You have to keep moving—just put on your mud boots and tromp on through it!

- **LUCINDA ROONEY,** *floral and garden designer:* If I had it to do over again the one thing I would focus more on is the structure of the business. You have to protect yourself; elicit mentors. Make sure you have a very experienced attorney.

you need to keep in mind as you plan. As for actually preparing the document, an Internet search or visit to your local office-supply store will turn up templates galore, but bath-and-body product creator Nyakio Kamoche Grieco suggests you approach your business plan the old-fashioned way—from scratch.

"For me, writing a business plan from scratch was the best way to know every aspect of my business," she says. "If I'd just been entering numbers in a form, I never would have grasped the concept of return on investment or learned how to make a company profitable. From the executive summary to my projections, doing it myself gave me the opportunity to sit down and really think out where I wanted the business to go."

BE VISIONARY AND CONCRETE

Writing a business plan forces you to confront the realities of your dream. This may be painful, but it's ultimately to your advantage. Be prepared to do a balancing act. You want to be true to yourself and your vision; if you write a plan that reflects what you think investors or colleagues want to hear, you may find yourself the owner of someone else's idea of your dream. On the other hand, remind yourself to stay realistic and conservative with your financial forecasts; if you do better than anticipated, you'll look stellar.

Once you've done a draft, solicit feedback from people whose opinion you respect. Bring your plan to one of the many SBA offices, where experienced advisers are available to give you an objective assessment.

BE FLEXIBLE

Heed the feedback you get from others. Don't get so attached to your plan that you fail to recognize its shortcomings or won't see and seize opportunities that may come along. Your plan is a map; be aware of and open to the detours.

✳ FIVE ESSENTIALS OF ✳ EVERY BUSINESS PLAN

1. BEGIN WITH A STATEMENT OF PURPOSE. You should be able to explain your business in twenty-five words or less.

2. EXPLAIN HOW YOUR BUSINESS WILL WORK. Explain why it will succeed.

3. FILL IN THE BUSINESS DETAILS. Describe its products or services, the customers, the market, and the competition. List the owners and managers and their credentials.

4. SUPPLY THREE YEARS OF PROJECTED FINANCIAL STATEMENTS. Include income, loss, and cash-flow projections.

5. PROVIDE SUPPORTING DOCUMENTS, such as references from creditors and potential clients and suppliers, evidence of insurance, etc.

SCORE: Counselors to America's Small Business
Washington, D.C.

Financing

After the idea itself, the biggest issue in starting your own business is one of the scariest: money. How much will you need? Where will it come from? How will you manage it? You should have answered some of these questions as you developed your business plan, so now it's time to arrange for financing. Double-check your plans with a certified public accountant to be sure you understand the ramifications of handling the financial transactions that come with business ownership (see Get Professional Advice on page 155).

SEED MONEY

Most of the women featured in these pages used their own savings or borrowed relatively small amounts to launch the business they'd dreamed of. Marilyn Lysohir, for example, saved the proceeds from the sales of her wonderful sculptures to get Cowgirl Chocolates off the ground. Others borrowed from friends and family.

Liz Alpert Fay tells a common story: "When I started with rug hooking, I needed money to pay the fees for shows, which can be hefty. So I asked my father for loans for the first few, and I'd pay him back after each show. That's how I started out."

Or, as Kate Shifrin, who collaborates with her husband, explains, "I financed Come Flea with Me from personal savings, and occasionally we dipped into an equity line."

Alternatively, when Lisa Norris got a large unexpected order from Anthropologie—after she stopped panicking—she took the order to the bank where she got the funding she needed to fulfill it.

TWO TYPES OF FINANCING

If you've done your business plan homework, you know there are two types of financing: debt and equity. Equity financing, where an investor buys a share of the operation—and expects a high rate of return—is usually the route reserved for more mature operations. Although Nyakio Kamoche Grieco was able to convince a few investors that her bath-and-body line had terrific promise and secured start-up money, that's uncommon, especially for most craft-based businesses. And it may not be part of your dream because it means someone else owns part of your business.

There are a number of sources for debt financing—credit cards, loans from family and friends, banks, and government agencies such as the Small Business Administration (SBA)—and all have their pluses and minuses. Credit cards, while oh-so-easy to use, are also oh-so-expensive, particularly if the interest rates are rising . And the regular payments on a bank loan can be difficult to maintain for small, struggling businesses in cyclical, seasonal industries. However,

- **KATE SHIFRIN**, *Flea-market tour producer:* I used a credit card to extend payment to thirty days, but always with the understanding that I'd pay that bill in full.

- **MICHELLE JOY**, *floral and home stylist:* I've used a trade-and-barter system for a lot of things. Someone may be looking for something that I can do and we trade it out. I got plumbing that way. I did a wedding and got a beautiful back porch.

regular payments, even on small loans, help to establish a credit-worthy reputation—something that will put you in a good light should you need to borrow more in the future.

PITCH YOUR BUSINESS TO THE POTENTIAL LENDERS

As more and more women set up and run successful businesses, securing loans has become easier, and the SBA programs for women entrepreneurs are a big help; take advantage of them. Invest time in talking with potential investors, especially the loan officer at your local bank. Learn the mechanics of applying for a loan, and share your plans and dreams with everyone who might be able to help. Lenders look for the promise of success; if you have prepared your business plan properly and

present it with passion, you may gain their confidence and support. If you are able to invest some money of your own, you'll show them you consider your idea worthy of risk.

Kaari Meng, owner of the lifestyle emporium French General, has a unique take on bank loans: Get one when you don't need it. When starting her business she was unable to secure a loan, but several years down the road, the bank called her! "Even when you don't need one, think about the future, for when you get a big order or want to expand, and there it will be," she says.

Personal loans from family and friends also warrant a serious approach. And in this case, your pitch is likely to fall on ears that already believe in you. In fact, a loan from a family member may be the best bet: You remain in control of the business and you won't have to worry about time-consuming reporting responsibilities. However, even if it's your doting grandmother who's providing start-up funds, the transaction should be handled in a serious, professional manner, with your business plan as the basis for an agreement on terms. (Be clear: She can't pick the color for your spring line!)

No matter which type of financing you choose or where it comes from, being realistic about taking on debt will put you on the firmest ground. Cozbi Cabrera explains that as she grew her business from dolls to a clothing line, "I created another business plan to raise some money but wound up midstream making a decision not to do that and just make my way slowly." Taking a step back allowed her to see that she was still learning her market and that saddling herself with debt at that point would be a bad idea.

✳ GET PROFESSIONAL FINANCIAL ADVICE ✳

Find a certified public accountant you trust and enjoy working with and ask:

- DO I HAVE ENOUGH MONEY? Don't enter into any legal, binding agreements or make investment decisions you cannot afford.

- WHICH BUSINESS ENTITY BEST SUITS MY NEW BUSINESS VENTURE: a sole proprietorship, corporation, S-corporation, partnership, or limited liability company (LLC)?

- WHICH TAXES AND INSURANCE TYPES MUST I PLAN FOR? There are income taxes, sales and use taxes, payroll taxes, workers' compensation insurance, disability insurance, liability insurance, and more.

- WHAT ARE PROPER BOOKKEEPING TECHNIQUES? A good accountant can help set up a system that works best for you, an essential for successful business management.

Janice Yahr, CPA
Yahr & Lally, Ronkonkoma, New York

Product Development

Your friends have been telling you for years you should be selling your work, or perhaps your first steps toward creativity have given you the confidence to take the leap. Whatever brought you to this point, there are a host of decisions to be made: What are you going to make and how will you make it? Where will you sell it and to whom? How will you protect your work?

CHOOSE YOUR NICHE

Do Web searches on your product and market. As SBA administrator Cheryl Mills points out on page 149, the first step in launching a business is learning your market and how to meet it. Success rests on not only an outstanding product but also an accessible market: Who's going to buy your product and where are they? That combination of product and market should be your starting point.

Read everything you can get your hands on. Take courses at your local community college. Go to craft fairs, trade shows, and every studio tour in your area, and everywhere you go, ask

questions. Look for a mentor to guide you and point out potential pitfalls.

When determining whether or not to add a particular design to her product line, paper designer Barbara Schriber considers four factors: uniqueness in the marketplace, ease of manufacturing, ideal price point, and what she calls "the pain-in-the-butt factor. "Something can be fabulous," she says, "but if it is a pain in the butt to make, I usually don't market it."

METHOD OF PRODUCTION

Will your product be handmade or will you work with a manufacturer? Perhaps your idea is something you

can license. For high-end items, reproductions may be a profitable option.

If your product is handmade, will it
be one-of-a-kind pieces or production
work? Some people, like rug designer
Crispina ffrench, find the repetition of
production work soothing. "I have this
idiot-savant kind of thing with pattern,
numbers, and repetition. I love production sewing," she says. Others, however, find it stifling.

Some artisans discover that their
singular handcrafted pieces lead to
exciting sidelines in commissioned
work. Denise Carpentier finds per-
sonalized requests for her pearlware
extremely satisfying. "People get so
excited that I'd do this for them that
I get excited too, and it's some of my
best work," she says.

One-of-a-kind pieces can be exhilarating for the artist but they also have
to sell, and that can be tricky. "Some
artists don't like the idea of money
dictating their creativity," says weaver
Phyllis Leck. "But I see it as a challenge; I want people to be able to
afford my work, want it, and appreciate it, all at the same time."

PRICING

Although it may seem counterintu-
itive, how much to sell your product

for is one of the first questions to think
about, not the last. If your product
can't be sold for more than you've put
into it, you need to rethink your plan.
The cost of your materials and labor,
your overhead (operating expenses
such as rent, utilities, and insurance),
and your selling expenses all must be
factored into your price.

✳ DEVELOPMENT ✳ CHECKLIST

Your business is like a puzzle;
refine the pieces until they fit
together.

- Find the unique selling point
  of your product.

- Figure out how to produce it
  efficiently in a way you enjoy.

- Price it so the customer can
  afford to purchase it and you
  can make a profit.

- Choose the kind of marketplace that's right for your
  business style: wholesale,
  retail, etc.

- Be nimble, be quick—if you
  can't change, your business
  won't grow.

- Protect your creativity and
  investment with solid legal
  advice.

Lamp-shade maker—and former accountant—Gloria Lombard explains, "When I buy my fabric, I record the price, and when I'm cutting the lamp shade out, I think, 'Okay, this design takes so many yards, and I'll get this many shades.' Then you have to take into account how many hours it took to make that product and you have to pay yourself." That means factoring in all the time you spend on an item, not just that of its actual production.

Setting prices correctly can make or break a fledgling operation. When Barbara Schriber began working with sales reps to augment her trade-show sales, "I had to reprice everything to absorb the commissions, and a lot of my customers got upset," she recounts. "I found I'd made a huge mistake with the initial pricing of one item, pricing it at what I thought the market could bear, not what I needed," she explains. "Well, it was a huge seller, but at a loss! When I sat down and determined my true costs I had to increase the price 50 percent."

Adds rug hooker Liz Alpert Fay, "I've periodically raised my prices, and because I'm out there selling my work, I get feedback from people. When I introduce something new, I ask people what they think of the price. I look around at what other people are charging, how long it takes me to do things, and what I think it's worth. I try to be really honest about that."

THE MARKETPLACE

What you make, how it's made, and the price point combine to determine the best place to sell your product. The options are dizzying. Many of the women profiled in these pages began, as did Anna Corba, simply by opening their studio doors or getting on an artist's tour. A number, like Lisa Norris and Lori Mitchell, started at gift and trade shows, and some, as Barbara did, went on to getting sales representatives to handle their lines. Nyakio's bath-and-body line and Jane Zaccaria's children's clothing are sold in retail outlets serviced by sales reps and online at their and other Web sites.

Other options are the art and craft fairs and antique shows, of varying levels of prestige, that take place all over the United States. Gloria Lombard, for example, plans her year's work around certain shows, such as the fabulous antiques show at Brimfield, Massachusetts. Photographer Hannah Gray built her reputation after being accepted by juried shows where committees of respected members in the field review applicants on

✳ THE INSIDE TRACK ✳

- JULIE DOBIES, *painter:* Don't forget that part of your price includes intangibles such as your style and experience.

- GLORIA LOMBARD, *handmade lamp shades:* Don't undervalue yourself and what you are doing. It's hard sometimes for crafters, especially women, to put a monetary value on that three hours it took to make something, but unless you are independently wealthy you have to. In addition to all the overhead costs you have to think, "What is a reasonable amount for me to make?"

- AMY BUTLER, *pattern and fabric designer:* Be inquisitive—networking is key to finding out how to do the things that scare you.

- ANNA CORBA, *vintage ephemera creator:* My market research is talking to my sales reps: What are people saying? Why isn't this moving?

- COZBI CABRERA, *doll maker and clothing designer:* I think there is such a thing as marketplace permission. The marketplace has to give you permission; if no one thinks your things are phenomenal, you really can't continue.

- LIZ ALPERT FAY, *rug hooker:* Some people don't like the restrictions of doing commissions but I love working with people, and a custom product becomes part of their lives—and then they come back. More and more I'm getting repeat business, and I really appreciate that.

- LORI MITCHELL, *folk artist:* Going through the contractual process for the reproduction of my work with a lawyer has been very helpful to me. I realize I've built something up, and I have to protect it.

the basis of such criteria as technical skill, creativity, medium, etc.

Representation by a well-known gallery is often a turning point in an artist's career, as it was for folk artist Denise Allen. Phyllis Leck is part of a cooperative gallery, where a number of artisans share space and responsibilities. And some artists, like Hannah Gray and Denise Allen, run their own galleries. And then, of course, there are the classic brick-and-mortar retail outlets such as Michelle Joy's florist shop and Cozbi Cabrera's dress shop.

Where you sell your product will change as you grow, but the more you know from day one, the better.

CHANGE IS GOOD!

Being an entrepreneur means being flexible and always thinking ahead. "It's a very fast-paced world," says Anna Corba, creator of vintage-inspired collages, "so in my mind, I'm always thinking about what I want to do next or where the color palette is going."

For Nyakio Kamoche Grieco, ideas for new product development "start anywhere, from waking up in the middle of the night dreaming about something, to asking questions like 'How is pumpkin or pomegranate good for the skin?'"

"Product development is my favorite," says Vicki Mote Bodwell. "I collected aprons at flea markets for years and thought they'd be cute for little girls, so we made them. They weren't selling at first because there wasn't enough of a story surrounding them, so we added a small stove and a tea set and a little cookbook." Sales took off, and when they added optional monogramming the aprons became a huge success.

For Kaari Meng, items she would like herself often become new products. "I used a line of candles in our New York store that became our signature scent, but I realized they gave off black soot. I researched it and learned that soy candles are much better for you, so we developed our own soy-wax candles with organic essential oils in the scents we wanted."

AN OUNCE OF PREVENTION . . .

After you've put your heart and soul into something (plus your life savings) make sure you're protected.

Designer Amy Butler has firsthand experience with this problem. "We get poached on a daily basis by people on eBay using my name and my patterns and fabric." Amy advises trademarking your company's name and all other things possible that identify your brand.

✳ CONSULT A LAWYER ✳

Find an attorney experienced with small business to guide you through these legal issues:

- LICENSING: Depending on your area and the nature of your operations, local (county, town, city, village) and state licensing may be required.

- PERMITS: Local laws regulate certain business operations. For example, many local governments require a permit for the operation of a home-based business.

- CONTRACTS: Be sure you understand the terms and conditions of all contracts so you assume rights and obligations specific to your business operations. As a start-up, you may have little room to negotiate. Try to build in a reasonable process for renegotiation when appropriate.

- INTELLECTUAL PROPERTY: Your work may involve designs, writing, trademarks, service marks, and domain name registrations for Web sites that need protection. State, federal, and even international laws may apply.

Marion Hancock Fish, Esq.
Hancock & Estabrook, LLP, Syracuse, New York

And if you are sending your work to another company for potential licensing, adds folk artist Lori Mitchell, "Absolutely do not send original work. I always send slides. Make sure your name is all over it and you have the copyright. Include return shipping."

Copyright forms can be downloaded from the Library of Congress. Consult your attorney about trademark questions. Is that wonderful name you've come up with already taken? "Come Flea with Me is a great name," says its creator, Kate Shifrin, "but there was a well-known company with a similar tagline," so she made sure there was no trademark infringement. A little time and money in research early on can avoid difficulty later, not to mention costly litigation!

Marketing and Sales

The tasks of marketing and selling your product are essentially the arts of defining, finding, and winning your customers. But at its most basic level, marketing is not so complicated. It's about people: meeting, telling, and selling them on you and your work. And since success so often rests on repeat business, marketing means creating an enjoyable experience that will encourage customers to return and send their friends to you as well.

Cozbi Cabrera puts it very well. "I think the starting point is listening to the customer," she says. "We often use the word *image* to refer to something slick, but it's simply a means of communicating an idea to the customer. It might be the choice of ribbon or tissue paper or even the choice of sticker. The logo. All the things customers take away are a reminder of their experience with our company."

YOUR LOOK

Your product may be terrific, but it isn't necessarily what your customer sees first. Your name, logo, Web site, signage, and displays all set the scene for the experience Cozbi describes.

Your "look" depends on how successfully and seamlessly these elements fit together to tell your story. Ask yourself: What am I selling? What colors, textures, and graphic style convey the essence of my business? Once you have the answer, then carry it all the way through—in your booth, catalog, shop, or Web site, and in the way you label and display your work or merchandise. A good graphic designer and photographer are essential for your look to be properly presented.

Seemingly small details can be vital, according to head of Cowgirl Chocolates, Marilyn Lysohir. "Last Christmas our PR firm, Serling & Associates, found beautiful wrapping paper," she says. "We found ribbons that worked and these little western buttons—little boots, stars, hats—that go on our fancy wrap and have since become a signature mark for our company. It branded us, the perfect touch that says it all."

"Branding is big," says French General's Kaari Meng. "Pick a simple name and a simple logo and stick with them; if you're going to make money people have to recognize you." French General features a plethora of offerings but Kaari explains, "as long as they always fit together in the same basket, so to speak, and look good, people will understand it."

MARKETING COMPONENTS

Once you've nailed your look, use it in as many ways as you can afford: on

---

✳ MARKETING ✳ CHECKLIST

Knowing your customer and how to reach him or her is key to your success; be creative, deliberate, and outgoing in your marketing endeavors.

- Create a visual identity for your business, an image that signals unmistakably the "brand" of your product or service.

- Invest in marketing materials— from hangtags and letterhead to brochures and a Web site— that exploit and reinforce your identity or brand.

- Create an effective Web site: Hire a creative and reliable designer who can help you conceive as well as maintain it.

- Use your site to gather contact information and spread the word about your business.

- Advertise in ways that will reach your customers and increase their numbers.

- Be ready at all times to promote your business and look for opportunities to do so— don't wait to be discovered.

business cards, postcards, hangtags, flyers, and shopping bags—even your invoices. Come up with a marketing plan and a budget. For your plan you'll want to consider a Web site and e-mail address, advertising, and publicity. And building alliances and relationships—networking—should be the cornerstone of your marketing efforts to get out your message.

YOUR WEB SITE: A 24/7, 365-DAYS-A-YEAR MARKETER

"A Web site is key," cake designer Elisa Strauss points out. "The first thing anyone does when they hear about a new business is check out its Web site." With the Internet used by the majority of the population and online sales reaching into the hundreds of billions of dollars, anyone with a product to sell should have a Web site. Visit other Web sites to gain insight into the ways yours can be effective, and check out Elements of a Winning Web Site, opposite.

Your Web site can be an important part of your selling arsenal or simply informational. Whichever function it serves, its design should be of a piece with the look you've developed so your customer is always aware and appreciative of where she is—you want your Web site to be a favorite destination. The Junk Gypsy site, www.gypsyville.com, is a very significant income source for its owners—so successful they've had to hire several employees just to keep up with the orders—but that wasn't its original purpose. "We battled one Web techie after another telling us we were doing everything wrong," says Jolie Sikes-Smith. "Amie and I thought the site should tell our story, inspire people, spread good karma, and 'Oh yeah, here's a T-shirt for sale'—and we were right, people really love it."

An e-commerce program can easily be added to any site. If you are selling items you create yourself, try starting online sales with pieces you make frequently, so stock will be easier to maintain, and factor online sales and fulfillment into your production schedule and overhead.

Even if a realistic assessment of your business tells you that for the foreseeable future your most lucrative outlet is still a particular show or event, you can use your site to enhance that income by holding a special online preview of what you'll be showing. Or launch a new product or new line on the site in the same manner.

✻ ELEMENTS OF A WINNING WEB SITE ✻

Web-site design is collaborative; tell your designer what you're looking for and listen when she shares her expertise. Make sure your site has:

- GREAT, FAST-LOADING, HIGH-RESOLUTION IMAGES of your work with well-lit, uncluttered backgrounds.

- THOUGHTFUL UP-TO-DATE CONTENT that portrays your style. Establish an affordable arrangement to update your site regularly or have it designed so that you can update it yourself.

- EASY NAVIGATION. Every page should provide a way back to the home page as well as your contact information.

- APPEAL! Put your site on everything from business cards to stickers. List it in directories, submit it to search engines, and collect e-mail addresses to keep in touch. Show off your talents even while you sleep.

Elizabeth Bashur
insight design studio, Pittsburgh, Pennsylvania

HIRING A WEB DESIGNER

Look at the sites of similar businesses—craftspeople working in your medium or a shop you admire—for ideas. Web designers are notorious for overbooking. Make sure yours isn't one of them by asking for time and schedule guarantees. "The thing I really love about my webmaster," says rug hooker Liz Alpert Fay, "is that he's a retired corporate executive and very accessible. I'm not that great at the computer, and having somebody who's reliable gives you a sense of security."

MAKE NEW FRIENDS AND KEEP THE OLD

Collect names and addresses (both land and e-mail) everywhere you go and use them. If you've set up your Web site to gather information from your visitors, you'll begin to build an e-mail list. (Be sure to include wording on all Web-based forms and lists indi-

✳ THE INSIDE TRACK ✳

- **KATE SHIFRIN,** *flea-market tour producer:* We had some great publicity, so we got numerous e-mails and phone calls from people asking to be on our mailing list. Next we'll purchase lists to target those who'd love our lifestyle trips.

- **COZBI CABRERA,** *doll maker and clothing designer, Cozbi Inc.:* When you care enough to think out even the smallest details surrounding your product, your customers notice and appreciate that.

- **MICHELLE JOY,** *floral and home stylist:* I think the best way to market yourself is to give yourself, to donate your time. I decorated a room for the local hospital's new cancer center. They paid the expenses only, but it will come back to me two-fold. It really gets your name out there.

- **LORI MITCHELL,** *folk artist:* My Web designer has been invaluable. He made sure my site looks good not just on my computers but on everyone's. Search engines are really a big thing, if people looking for your kind of product can't find you, your Web site is worthless.

- **PHYLLIS LECK,** *weaver:* A good Web site is a real time saver for artists. It cuts down on phone discussions because people get their questions answered online plus they can see what my work looks like, and I don't have to make and send so many samples.

cating that those signing up wish to be contacted by you and stating your privacy policy.) If you do shows or have a retail shop, make sure there's a way for people to add their names to your mailing list. Try a raffle at your booth or one day in your shop—have slips of paper for people to fill out, then draw names every few hours and give away something from your business.

Try an e-mail newsletter. (Have your Web designer do a template when she does your site.) Send out announcements about your latest work with e-mail–sized images. Participating in a show, open studio tour, or hosting your annual open house? Send an e-mail to all those on your list letting them in on it, perhaps with an exclusive "preview offer." Who knows, your most avid collector may be in Rangoon that week but see your e-mail and fire back an order for your newest offering.

DON'T GO IT ALONE

Your business may be such that doing all the selling yourself is too time-consuming or not the most effective way of reaching your customer. If you have a line of products, you may wish to use a showroom or sales representative; if you are an artist, a gallery may be essential. These people will take a commission on the sales they make (usually 15 to 20 percent), but they'll actively promote your work in order to earn it—which ultimately benefits you financially and frees your time and resources for other things.

"I do trade shows because I believe I represent my products best," says Anna Corba, vintage ephemera creator. "I know the line the best and people like to meet the person behind the products. And I always do well when I do the shows myself. The down side of a rep or showroom is you're one of twenty-five lines, and they can't give yours all the attention because they don't have time. That's why I do both: do some trade shows myself and work with reps as well."

Ways to find a showroom or rep include networking with peers, querying the management of wholesale trade shows (some of whom maintain showrooms), and searching the Internet. Another good resource is the ads in trade publications—both the classified and those for other craftspeople's work; the latter of which often cite a rep or showroom contact. An important consideration when choosing a rep is the territory he or she covers; you may need more than one to gain exposure in several different markets. A wide territory was one of the things that drew Barb Schriber to the rep she chose for her paper goods.

ADVERTISING AND PUBLICITY

Advertising is expensive, but even if your business is a modest one you can use it effectively if you know your customers and their media habits. Having an opening or a sale? How about placing an ad in the local paper or on the campus Web site? That quarter inch of print or a Web banner ad can work if you've got something special to say and say it well.

Direct mail is another option. It's costly, but, especially if your product is visually appealing or looks like fun, it may be worth the investment to create postcards, invitations, brochures, or a catalog and send them to established as well as potential customers. "Marketing for us is almost completely direct mail," says service-business owner Kate Shifrin of Come Flea with Me. To expand your market, you may wish to rent a "list" of potential customers from a broker, or perhaps you can trade information with someone in a similar business endeavor. If you do the latter, be sure you've cleared the right to share their contact information with your customers; you don't want to alienate them. Via either print or e-mail, contacting your target customer directly is a great idea.

And never underestimate word of mouth, particularly in some industries and areas of the country. Interior decorator Marcia Gottlieb firmly believes her long success rests on personal referrals by clients to their friends.

SHAMELESS SELF-PROMOTION

It is worth noting that one of the threads running through the stories gathered here is the pivotal role played by publicity, sometimes at a key moment. For the majority of these entrepreneurs the big break took the form of some kind of publicity: a newspaper, magazine, or television story that either gave them the confidence to continue or actually took the business to a new level.

Connections can be a huge advantage, but what characterizes every successful entrepreneur is an eye for an opening. "I did everything I could do to be prepared when opportunity came," says garden designer Lucinda Rooney, "and luck has nothing to do with it! If you want to get somewhere, you have to ask for it."

Have a press or marketing kit (your business card, a photo and/or catalog, and your biography) always at the ready. Julie Dobies took her marketing kit to a trade show and won a contract for her high-quality prints. You never know when a reporter looking for a story may wander into your booth at a show. But don't wait for that moment. Go find it! Following the suggestions in Getting the Word Out, below, makes a good start. Be proactive and use every opportunity to build your network of contacts.

✳ GETTING THE WORD OUT ✳

If nobody knows about your outstanding product or service, it doesn't do you much good. Here are a few tips to get you noticed:

- **DEFINE YOUR TARGET MARKET** and make an emotional connection beyond the product or service.

- **COMMUNICATE YOUR UNIQUENESS** and know the competitive advantage of your product or service.

- **EMBRACE YOUR BRAND WITH PASSION** and understand it clearly. You'll infuse others with your enthusiasm.

- **GET YOUR PRODUCT INTO THE HANDS OF THE MEDIA** and relevant decision makers whenever possible.

- **PITCH YOUR STORY TO THE APPROPRIATE MEDIA CONTACT.** Outline three key messages about your brand. Be succinct and factual. Always have a news angle, and respect the reporter's time.

Sandi Serling, President
Serling & Associates, Inc., Lake Oswego, Oregon

come flea with me
market dates 2007

april 22 sandwich, il
may 20 elkhorn, wi
june 24 allegan, mi
july 29 rosemont, il
aug 25 wheaton, il all niter
sept 15 wilmette/lake bluff, il
oct 9 london, england

COLOURPICTURE™ PUBLICATIO

CONFETTI CAKES
www.confetticakes.com

New York, New York

(212) 877-9580

Elisa Strauss
Custom Cakes By Appointm

tiddlywinks & scallywags

PR
A
Garden
An eclect
for the
Finer Flow
Vint
Cotta
Open Wit
Grove
Route 9,

ANNA CORBA
ound Cat Studio

Sonoma Ridge Rd.
a Rosa, CA 95404
707)   FAX (707)
340   544·0357

me fle

llen's General S
And Folk Art Gallery

F
Ge

HO
T

Napkins
Shower
Bath S

Julie A. Dobies
FINE ART

amy
butler

SUMMER'S DAYDREAM

lisa norris
owner/artist

inspire big dreams...
Warm Biscuit
bedding company

Barbara Schriber
DESIGNS INC

0" × 48"

made by one girl
www.madebyonegirl.com
1614 south seminole dri
chattanooga, tenn 37412
23.867.3360

* Presenting Your Vision

First impressions can be lasting ones, so you want them to be positive and strong. Whatever the nature of your business, the graphic materials you use to represent it should reflect the style and spirit of your product, be of a piece, and be the best you can afford to create. The better conceived and designed your logo, stationery, business cards, labels, packaging, catalogs, and brochures the more seriously your business will be taken and the more professional you'll feel. Here are examples from some of the businesses profiled in this book. Whether traditional or off-beat, quiet or vivacious, these printed materials communicate with verve and distinctive style.

Financial Management

According to the Small Business Administration, among the top ten reasons new businesses fail are poor record keeping and financial controls and lack of experience in running a business. Keeping full, detailed records (and every receipt!) is essential, textile designer Liz Alpert Fay says. You can only see the progress and know the current condition of your business with accurate and timely financial reports.

Floral designer Michelle Joy learned this the hard way when she discovered her trusted bookkeeper was pocketing some of the proceeds! Since no one alerted her, she just assumed everything was okay. No longer. "Once a month sit down and look at everything," Michelle advises, "the receipts, all the checks dispersed, your bank statement. My biggest lesson to date was not paying attention to the important things."

There's a tried-and-true business adage for time management: Devote one third of your time to creativity, one third to marketing, and one third to the management of your business. Take a deep breath and dig in.

BUDGETS AND STATEMENTS AND BILLS, OH MY!

Once you're open for business the bills start arriving, and what you're owed needs to be collected so you can pay the bills and yourself (see The Basics of Accounts Payable and Receivable, page 175). "Accounts payable and receivable can be a real headache," concedes tiddlywinks & scalliwags founder Jane Zaccaria, "but because I've always wanted to keep a handle on things, like who's buying and what they're buying, being a hands-on manager has been helpful to me."

Crispina ffrench, who's been running her own business for over fifteen years (and she's only forty), agrees. "It's important to understand what goes into making a business function on a day-to-day basis."

Work with your accountant to set up standardized methods and appropriate forms to facilitate the smooth running of your business. You'll want to monitor the three major financial reports: the *balance sheet* (the simple formula is Assets = Owner's Equity – Liabilities); the *profit-and-loss statement* (P&L), which measures a company's sales and expenses over a specific period of time; and the *cash-flow statement* (cash received and cash

---

✳ FINANCIAL ✳ MANAGEMENT CHECKLIST

It's your business; keep track of the money

- Keep good records of every transaction, be it expense or sale.

- Learn to make and understand the three major financial reports; they indicate the health of your business.

- Set aside money for taxes, and pay them when due.

- Carry the proper insurance.

---

expended for each month of the year). Keep all of these up-to-date.

Use the P&L statements to create your budget—the cold-numbers equivalent of your business plan. Can you afford to move beyond your home-based location, buy new equipment, or hire needed staff? The budget tells you what's actually possible, not just what you'd like to hear.

TAXES AND INSURANCE

Of course, there are always taxes and insurance. Crispina says, "When I started out I never even considered

- **CRISPINA FFRENCH,** *rug and accessory designer:* Operating a business without liability insurance is like driving a car without insurance. It might not be illegal, but it's really dumb.

- **JOLIE SIKES-SMITH,** *apparel and accessories retailer:* Since we started with only $2,000, we organically built the business by something real simple: Don't spend it if you don't have it!

- **ANNA CORBA,** *vintage ephemera creator:* I don't extend myself beyond what I'm asked to do; I'm not willing to take that risk. I create a modest line of what I'm going to present. I go out and get my orders, I come back home, I buy what I need, I make the orders, and I ship them off. I've never gotten in over my head—that's been a huge saving grace for me.

insurance, but you really need it." If someone comes to your studio and injures her- or himself, you can be sued and end up losing your business, she points out. "When you have employees," she continues, "taxes are a huge thing. When you figure out how much you're paying somebody to make something, you've got to add a third for taxes. Workers compensation, liability insurance—they're part of the hidden costs involved in a business. My advice, particularly for someone who hasn't been trained in business, is to understand the hidden costs involved in business and to learn what goes into making that business function on a day-to-day basis."

Your accountant should advise you on which taxes you're subject to and on what and how much insurance you need to carry. Even if you work alone, you have to pay taxes on whatever you take out of the business, whether it's as a salary or profit. It's a good idea to check with your lawyer about tax liability and insurance too, because the scale of your enterprise and the form in which you establish it affect your responsibilities in these matters.

✳ THE BASICS OF ✳
ACCOUNTS PAYABLE AND RECEIVABLE

The goal is to hold on to your cash as long as possible without annoying your suppliers while getting your customers to pay as quickly as you can.

For paying bills

- Use a credit card to extend your cash flow—and possibly earn bonus points for free items.

- Use the online bill-payment service offered by most banks, saving both postage and time.

- Pay your bills on time—not early but not so late that your suppliers become irritated.

- Don't automatically pay every bill that comes your way. Check to make sure that the bill is legitimate, that it's for what you ordered, that the pricing is accurate, and that you have not already paid for the goods.

For collections

- Accept payment by credit card, especially if you're concerned about your customer's financial stability.

- Don't wait until the end of the month to send bills. Your bill date should be the same as your ship date.

- Follow up immediately on all past-due bills. Let your customers know you expect to be paid on time.

- Make sure your customers know your payment terms *before* you deliver your product.

Mary S. Schaeffer
Editorial director, Accounts Payable Now & Tomorrow,
author of Essentials of Credit, Collections, and Accounts Receivable
Newark, Delaware

Staffing

This is yet another of those business aspects that can be painfully difficult. But in any successful venture the day arrives when its founder is confronted with the necessity of hiring help.

For Elisa Strauss each cake is a unique creation and she has a hand in every one. "When you start out doing everything yourself, you have to learn to let go. I don't need more business; I need to take me out of the equation." This can be wrenching. After all, it's hard to give up control of something that's so close to your heart.

WHAT'S REALLY NEEDED?

The first thing to determine is what's really needed: full-time, part-time, or seasonal help. For many artisans, production is cyclical. Some simply need help with packing and shipping while others need skilled assistants, seamstresses, or business managers.

Just as important as knowing your strengths is identifying areas in which you could use some help. For example, if your math skills are a family joke, hiring a bookkeeper might be the smartest staffing decision for you.

When Lori Mitchell wanted to expand her business she thought she'd figured out a division of labor for making her handcrafted, hand-painted papier-mâché figures, but implementing it was another story. "It takes a long time for somebody to get up to speed and start helping you. I knew that going in, but what I didn't realize was how much work it meant for me." She found herself staying up half the night just to keep the work flowing. Her solution? Partnering with a manufacturer to make reproductions of her charming originals.

Amy Butler explains that staffing for her fabric design and sewing-pattern business can be a challenge. "When we're creating new patterns, we back up three months and figure out what needs to happen each week to test the patterns and get them to market. Then we start calling all our local ladies and say, 'We've got this going on, are you interested?'" She has to be flexible, Amy says, because the cost of a full-time staff of seamstresses would be prohibitive.

FINDING HELP

Word of mouth is often a great way to solve your staffing needs. Anna Corba says, "Staffing is hard because some months I'm busy and some months I'm not." She finds help with her collaged accessories by calling her contacts or by pinning a notice on the bulletin board at the local college.

A growing number of small businesswomen use interns, usually paid, as a strategy or as a first step in figuring out staffing needs. When the head of the MBA program at nearby Pace University suggested to Vicki Mote Bodwell that she get an intern, she did. "We've gotten the most incredible people from Pace, so I'm a huge advocate of student interns," says Vicki.

✳ **STAFFING** ✳
CHECKLIST

Needing help is a good sign—it means that your business is growing. Before hiring, think about what kind of staff will keep your business healthy and enable you to do the things you're best at and enjoy the most.

- Decide whether you need full-time, part-time, or occasional, seasonal help.

- Determine which tasks your employees will perform and what skills they should have.

- Network and advertise to find the right help.

- Manage as you would like to be managed, but keep your authority clear and don't be so caring you find yourself being the mother.

"You can identify people you want to hire," she suggests, and several former interns are now on her staff.

NEAREST AND DEAREST

"Don't hire family or friends" say the warnings, but a number of our artisan mentors turn that conventional staffing wisdom on its head. Of her partnership with her husband, David, Amy Butler says, "We have a house rule that we don't talk about work after work. We leave the studio—it's on the bottom level of our house—between five and six o'clock every night, and that's it."

Lisa Norris reports that when she went through a rough patch in managing her growing business, she called on her friends for advice. One friend volunteered to work with her for free. "Now she is on salary," Lisa reports. "We got my business organized with a better cash flow. It just started with me making phone calls to all my friends."

"Support from my family and friends has been key to my getting where I am," says potter Denise Carpentier. At shows, family members help her set up and break down the booth, friends stand in so she can visit other booths, a niece wraps the purchases, and her mom brings lunch. For so many entrepreneurs, networking comes through again and again.

MANAGING

Almost all of us have functioned in the employee role, an experience to remember in your role of employer. The best approach is to manage as you would want to be managed. How you function in this capacity will set the tone for your company; it's what defines "corporate culture."

Managing staff was hard for Cozbi Cabrera at first. "I'd decide to whip up something to eat and ask the embroiderers if they wanted some, and before I knew it I was cooking for my staff." She's since learned you can be a fair and generous human being "without adopting everybody."

Chocolatier Marilyn Lysohir also has learned from her experiences at the helm of a growing business. "I think you have to be not only a leader but also a team player," she says. "I'm the head cowgirl. I never look down my nose at any job. I'll run the sweeper; I'll clean the toilet."

Staffing decisions can be pivotal. "I could not have grown without delegating to my staff and trusting them," says Barbara Schriber. "If I were to micromanage, check every detail, and make sure everything's done exactly the way I want, I'd never do anything but production."

What's the bottom line? "Role changes are hard for people," Crispina ffrench points out. "The important thing is to establish clear guidelines on what you expect of people" (see Learn to Manage and Motivate, below). She's right. Only within that framework can everyone in your organization be motivated and grow with you.

✳ LEARN TO MANAGE AND MOTIVATE ✳

Your passion for your business is a given. Here are some tips for creating an enthusiastic and committed staff who support it.

- BE SPECIFIC when you define your assistants' responsibilities and clear about your expectations.

- KEEP YOUR STAFF INFORMED about the business and let them share in the decision making.

- BE APPROACHABLE and stay tuned to the workplace atmosphere. Listen. Reward good ideas and address morale problems promptly.

- ACKNOWLEDGE GOOD WORK, and reward it the best way you can. Keep criticism constructive; it should never be personal.

- DON'T MICROMANAGE; trust your staff to perform the task you've outlined. But don't let things slip either. Stay on top of the situation.

- BE AWARE OF STRENGTHS AND WEAKNESSES. Let people flourish and don't force them down paths they're not suited to follow.

Growing Bigger

What is meant by growing bigger? Does it mean producing more, selling more, or making different or more expensive products? A great question. Growth can mean many different things, and you need to determine what's appropriate for your business and your personal philosophy.

The first year of a new business is an intensive educational and emotional experience—an MBA program you didn't know you'd signed up for. And growth—examining it, planning it, and managing it—is the last seminar before graduation.

WAYS TO GROW

Growth can mean hiring someone to take over certain business responsibilities, as Lisa Norris did when one of her close friends came on board to handle business management.

Here's another scenario. Following an appearance in *Country Living*, several options opened up for Gloria Lombard's lamp shade business. Contacted by a number of shops interested in carrying her shades, she decided to give wholesaling a shot. After cal-culating her wholesale discount (the price at which she sells to a retailer, who then marks it up roughly 33 percent), she had to think about placement. "You can be overexposed," she points out, if your product is in too many stores. She also realized she needed a real Web site and at least one person to do some of the basic cutting and gluing so she has more time to make lamp shades.

One of the first steps an expanding small business often takes is the one

Cowgirl Chocolates took: moving out of Marilyn Lysohir's sunroom—with boxes of chocolate filling the hot tub—into its own 1,500-square-foot space with an office, packing/shipping area, and a shop. "We handle fulfillment, and we'd gotten a really big order. We were tripping over boxes and I thought, 'This isn't going to work any more,'" Marilyn recalls. "The shop is a whole new ball game for us." Marilyn is an accomplished artist as well as a chocolatier, so in addition to the luscious sweets, her fine art is on display in the shop (see page 86).

Liz Alpert Fay looks to her new studio as a growth vehicle for her hooked rug business. "The way I hook is very spontaneous. It's not the kind of thing somebody else could do and have it look the same. But I certainly could have people sew for me—something I don't have room for now—and increase my production capacity."

Expanding product lines is another way to grow. For artisans whose originals come with high price tags, lower-priced reproductions can be a great addition. Folk artist Denise Allen listened when her customers asked for prints of her colorful collaged scenes, picking "some of the pieces that I really liked and people responded to"

✳ GROWTH ✳ CHECKLIST

Your business will no doubt tell you when it's ready to expand. Seize the opportunity in a way that's right for you.

- Define the way in which you want to grow: Add staff? Expand your product line? Segue into an ancillary product or related venture? Change your business format to retail shop or wholesale? License your work? Move to a larger facility?

- Keep the growth sustainable. Don't finance your expansion with unwarranted debt.

- Be patient; give yourself time to succeed and to figure out the best changes for you.

- Keep your mission and goals in mind and make sure you'll still have the job of your dreams.

---

for limited edition prints. Then she signed a contract with the company making the prints to also sell them.

Denise has another new product that brings her full cycle. "I started out with embroidery, and now I'm making embroidery kits," she reports. She has photographs of her work put on fabric for the kits and thinks she'll be able to reach a wider market.

Ancillary products created in addition to the primary venture—Sisters on the Fly founder Maurrie Sussman's cowgirl bedding, for example—is another option.

One of the truisms of business development is that it takes you places you never expected. Judy Godwin, her antique business sidelined by a car accident, uses her stock of classic linens, silver, and antique serving pieces to add elegance to her growing catering business. Cake designer Elisa Strauss and garden designer Lucinda Rooney have moved into publishing and television. While your business— just like your life—can take you in unplanned directions, it is the sum of your past experiences that provides the foundation for your next undertaking. When checking in with your business plan to measure how you're doing on the numbers front, use the opportunity to ask yourself where you want to be as a creative person six months or a year from now.

SUSTAINABLE

Resist the advice—or temptation—to leverage yourself too soon, advises doll maker Cozbi Cabrera. (Leverage is the amount of debt used to finance your venture's assets.) "You can wind up making decisions that aren't in the best interest of your company simply to satisfy the debt." If you grow your business organically, she believes, it may be a little slower going, but you can better direct its course.

Vicki Mote Bodwell has a similar philosophy. "Sustainable profit and growth should always be your goal. Never forget that," she says. "Is the goal to be like the hundred-million-dollar Pottery Barn? Maybe not. You want to be big but at the same time continue to have fun."

Janie Sikes and daughters Amie and Jolie, the Junk Gypsies, have been besieged with offers of TV series, books, and products as their popularity has grown, but they've reacted cautiously. "We want to stay true to who we are, who our customers are, and how we started the business," says Jolie. "We've been taking it all in, trying to figure out what the right thing to do is," adds Amie, "and who's the right person to do it with."

WHAT'S BEST FOR YOU?

"I have purposely kept my business this manageable size," says Anna Corba, "because I truly still like to

- CRISPINA FFRENCH, *rug and accessory designer:* Fresh product, fresh sales keep it going. Our look is recognizable and that's great, but the flip side is it can go out of fashion so we always have to be creative. Don't get stuck in one place; what's working today may not work tomorrow.

- AMY BUTLER, *pattern and fabric designer:* A new relationship or new product needs to fit our criteria. Both need to be a good fit with our brand. We look at our opportunities with a checklist: How do we feel about this specific company? How do we feel about this specific goal? It's also about doing our homework and having all the contracts in place legally. It's easy to get burned when you're starting out.

- ELISA STRAUSS, *cake designer:* At one point I had seven people working for me, and I realized I was just taking on more and more work to justify their salaries. I wasn't making any more money and I was still working on every single cake. Every cake we do is different, and I never want to be like other businesses mass-producing cakes. That's why I'm looking toward books and television.

have my hands on my pieces. I am not at the point where I just want to design and then pass it off to six people who make them."

Each of you will have a different answer to the challenge of growth, deciding to develop certain products you can sell in quantity, or choosing to create unique items that individual customers search out and claim as *theirs.* Whichever direction you go, you'll balance your creative dream with financial reality to achieve the kind of success that is right for you. Your route on that road map to success should include whichever straight paths, detours, stops, and observation points create a truly satisfying experience for you. Isn't that what crafting your business is all about?

RESOURCES

Marki McMillan and
Rae Lynn White
Franciska's House
La Grange, TX 78945
(713) 861-5921

Kaari Meng
French General
1621 Vista Del Mar
Hollywood, California 90028
(323) 462-0818 (10–5 PCT)
www.frenchgeneral.com

Lori Mitchell
La Dee Dah Folk Art
3309 Kensington Avenue
Richmond, VA 23221
www.ladeedahfolkart.com
(804) 342-1809

Lisa Norris
Made By One Girl
1614 South Seminole Drive
Chattanooga, TN 37412
www.madebyonegirl.com
(423) 867-3360

Lucinda Rooney
Lucinda Rooney, LLC
P.O. Box 286
Middlebury, VT 05753
www.lucindarooney.com
(802) 545-2562

Barbara Schriber
Barbara Schriber Designs, Inc.
615 Baldy Mountain Road
Sandpoint ID 83864
www.barbaraschriberdesigns.com
(208) 255-7741

Kate Shifrin
Come Flea with Me
6153 West Mulford, Unit D
Niles, IL 60714
www.comefleawithme.com
(773) 281-KATE (5283)

Amie Sikes, Janie Sikes,
Jolie Sikes-Smith
The Junk Gypsy Company
4345 Alexis Court
College Station, TX 77845
www.gypsyville.com
(979) 776-5151

Elisa Strauss
Confetti Cakes
102 West 87th Street
New York, NY 10024
(By appointment only)
www.confetticakes.com
(212) 877-9580

Maurrie Sussman
Sisters on the Fly
10231 North 39th Street
Phoenix, AZ 85028
www.sistersonthefly.com
(602) 996-4491;
cell: (602) 908-0680

Jane Zaccaria
tiddlywinks & scallywags
439 Pennsylvania Avenue
Glen Ellyn, IL 60137
www.britkid.com
(630) 545-2715

PROFESSIONAL
DIRECTORY

Elizabeth Bashur
insight design studio
938 Haslage Avenue
Pittsburgh, PA 15212
www.insightdesignstudio.com
(412) 606-7520

Marion Hancock Fish
Hancock & Estabrook, LLP
1500 Tower I, P.O. Box 4976
Syracuse, NY 13221
www.hancocklaw.com
(315) 471-3151, ext. 382

Cheryl A. Mills,
Associate Deputy Administrator
Office of Entrepreneurial
Development
U.S. Small Business
Administration
409 Third Street SW, 6th floor
Washington, DC 20416
www.sba.gov
(202) 401-5004

Mary Schaeffer
*Accounts Payable Now &
Tomorrow*
560 Peoples Plaza #197
Newark, DE 19702
www.ap-now.com
(302) 836-0540

SCORE: Counselors to
America's Small Business
409 Third Street SW, 6th floor
Washington, DC 20024
www.score.org
(800) 634-0245

Sandi Serling
Serling & Associates, Inc.
14495 Fosberg Road
Lake Oswego, OR 97035
(503) 697-0649

Janice M. Yahr, CPA
Yahr and Lally
3505 Veterans Memorial
Highway #N
Ronkonkoma, NY 11779
(631) 737-2080

MENTORS' RESOURCES

The following resources are
suggested by the women
profiled in this book.

Craft Associations/
Trade Organizations

The American Ceramic
Society
735 Ceramic Place, suite 100
Westerville, OH 43081
www.ceramics.org
(866) 721-3322

American Craft Council
72 Spring Street
New York, NY 10012
www.craftcouncil.org/
(212) 274-0630
Membership includes subscrip-
tion to American Craft Magazine;
reference library; craft shows

Americans for the Arts
1000 Vermont Avenue NW,
6th floor
Washington, DC 20005
(202) 371-2830
New York City Office
One East 53rd Street, 2nd floor
New York, NY 10022
www.artsusa.org
(212) 223-2787
Advocacy and professional
organization

American Society of
Interior Design
608 Massachusetts Avenue NE
Washington, DC 20002
www.asid.org
(202) 546-3480
Professional educational
organization

Apparel Industry Board Inc.
(AIBI)
350 West Mart Center Drive,
suite 690, Chicago, IL 60654
www.aibi.com
(312) 836-1041
Fashion industry organization

Craft Emergency Relief Fund
P.O. Box 838
Montpelier, VT 05601
www.craftemergency.org
(802) 229-2306
Advocacy and relief organization

Furniture Society
111 Grovewood Road
Asheville, NC 28804
www.furnituresociety.org
(828) 255-1949

Glass Art Society
3131 Western Avenue, suite 414
Seattle, WA 98121
www.glassart.org
(206) 382-1305

Handweavers Guild of
America
1255 Buford Highway, suite 211
Suwanee, GA 30024
www.weavespindye.org
(678) 730-0010

John Michael Kohler
Arts Center
608 New York Avenue
Sheboygan, WI 53081
www.jmkac.org
(920) 458-6144
Preeminent nonprofit arts and
crafts institution

Education

Arrowmont School of Arts
and Crafts
P.O. Box 567
Gatlinburg, TN 37738
www.arrowmont.org/
(423) 436-5860

Brookfield Craft Center
286 Whisconier Road
P.O. Box 122
Brookfield, CT 06804
www.brookfieldcraftcenter.org
(203) 775-4526

Center for Book Arts
28 West 27th Street, 3rd floor
New York, NY 10001
www.centerforbookarts.org
(212) 481-0295

Center for Craft, Creativity
& Design
University of North Carolina
Kellogg Center
1181 Broyles Road
P.O. Box 1127
Hendersonville, NC 28793
www.craftcreativitydesign.org
(828) 890-2050

Fashion Institute of
Technology
Seventh Avenue at 27th Street
New York, NY 10001
www.fitnyc.edu
(212) 217-7999

Greenwich House Pottery
16 Jones Street
New York, NY 10014
www.greenwichhouse.org
(212) 242-4106

Haystack Mountain School
of Crafts
P.O. Box 518
Deer Isle, ME 04627
www.haystack-mtn.org
(207) 348-2306

Penland School of Crafts
P.O. Box 37
Penland, NC 28765-0037
www.penland.org
(828) 765-2359

Touchstone Center for Crafts
1049 Wharton Furnace Road
Farmington, PA 15437
www.touchstone.com
(412) 329-1370

Business Associations/ Organizations

American Woman's Economic
Development Corporation
(AWED)
216 East 45th Street, 10th floor
New York, NY 10017
www.awed.org
(917) 368-6100

Business Networking
International
45 College Commerce Way
Upland, CA 91786
www.bni.com
(800) 825-8286

Online Women's Business
Centers
Small Business Administration
409 Third Street SW, 6th Floor
Washington, DC 20416
www.onlinewbc.gov
(202) 205-6673
Part of the SBA's
Entrepreneurial Development's
network of services

National Association of
Female Executives (NAFE)
260 Madison Avenue, 3rd floor
New York, NY 10016
www.nafe.com
(800) 927-6233

National Association of
Women Business Owners
8405 Greensboro Drive,
suite 800
McLean, VA 22102
www.nawbo.org
(800) 55-NAWBO
Advocacy and professional
membership organization

SCORE: Counselors to
America's Small Business
409 Third Street SW, 6th floor
Washington, DC 20024
www.score.org
(800) 634-0245
Free small business advice;
SBA partner

Small Business Administration
409 Third Street SW
Washington, DC 20416
www.sba.gov
(800) U-ASK-SBA

Springboard Enterprises
2100 Foxhall Road NW
Washington, DC 20007
(202) 242-6282
www.springboardenterprises.org
A nonprofit organization dedi-
cated to accelerating women's
access to the equity markets

WIBO (Workshop in Business
Opportunities)
220 East 23rd Street, room 309
New York, NY 10010
www.wibo.org
(212) 684-0854
Nonprofit corporation enabling
budding entrepreneurs in
underserved communities to
start, operate, and build
successful businesses

Women's Chamber of
Commerce
1201 Pennsylvania Avenue
NW, suite 300
Washington, DC 20004
www.sblink.us/html/uswcc.aspx
(888) 41-USWCC

Women's Venture Fund
240 West 35th Street, suite 201
New York, NY 10001
www.womensventurefund.org
(212) 563-0499
Nonprofit organization providing capital and mentorship to minority women entrepreneurs

Books

A Shop of One's Own: Women Who Turned the Dream into Reality, Rachel Epstein, Hearst Books

Crafting as a Business, Wendy Rosen, The Rosen Group

Good to Great: Why Some Companies Make the Leap . . . and Others Don't, Jim Collins, HarperCollins Publishers Inc.

Making a Living in Crafts, Donald A. Clark, Lark Books

Purple Cow: Transform Your Business by Being Remarkable, Seth Godin, Penguin Group (USA) Inc.

The Art of Possibility, Transforming Professional and Personal Life, Rosamund Stone Zander and Benjamin Zander, Harvard Business School Press

The Artist's Way, A Spiritual Path to Higher Creativity, Julia Cameron, Penguin Group (USA) Inc.

The Business of Bliss: How to Profit from Doing What You Love, Janet Allon and the editors of *Victoria Magazine*

The Creative Habit: Learn It and Use It for Life, Twyla Tharp, Simon & Schuster

The Do-It-Yourself Business Book, Gustav Berle, John Wiley & Sons

The E-Factor: Building a 24/7, Customer-Centric, Electronic Business for the Internet Age, Martin T. Focazio, AMACON

The Fashiondex, Apparel Industry Publishers, www.fashiondex.com. Fashion industry sourcebooks.

The Girl's Guide to Starting Your Own Business: Candid Advice, Frank Talk, and True Stories for the Successful Entrepreneur, Caitlin Friedman and Kimberly Yorio, HarperCollins Publishers Inc.

Turn Your Passion Into Profits: How to Start the Business of Your Dreams, Janet Allon and the editors of *Victoria Magazine,* Hearst Books

You Can Do It!: The Merit Badge Handbook for Grown-up Girls, Lauren Catuzzi Grandcolas, Chronicle Books

Magazines

Accessories Magazine
185 Madison Avenue, 5th floor,
New York, NY 10016
(212) 686-4412
www.accessoriesmagazine.com

American Craft Magazine
72 Spring Street,
New York, NY 10012
(212) 274-0630
www.craftcouncil.org
Free with membership in the American Craft Council

AmericanStyle Magazine
3000 Chestnut Avenue #300
Baltimore, MD 21211
(410) 889-3093
www.AmericanStyle.com

Art and Antiques
2100 Powers Ferry Road
Atlanta, GA 30339
(770) 955-5656
www.artantiquesmag.com

Art in America
575 Broadway
New York, NY 10012
(212) 941-2806
www.artinamericamagazine.com

Bust
P.O. Box 1016, Cooper Station
New York, NY 10276
(866) 220-6010,
www.bust.com

Country Living
300 West 57th Street
New York, NY 10019
www.countryliving.com

Entrepreneur
Entrepreneur Media Inc.
2445 McCabe Way, suite 400
Irvine, CA 92614
(949) 261-2325
www.entrepreneur.com

Niche
3000 Chestnut Avenue #300
Baltimore, MD 21211
(410) 889-3093
www.nichemag.com

Pottery Making Illustrated
735 Ceramic Place, suite 100
Westerville, OH 43081
(800) 340-6532
www.potterymaking.org
A publication of The American
Ceramic Society

Sunshine Artist
Palm House Publishing
4075 L.B. McLeod Road,
suite E
Orlando, FL 32811
(800) 597-2573
www.sunshineartist.com

Shuttle, Spindle & Dyepot
1255 Buford Highway,
suite 211
Suwanee, GA 30024
(678) 730-0010
www.weavespindye.org
Journal of the Handweavers
Guild of America

The Crafts Report
100 Rogers Road,
Wilmington, DE 19801
(800) 777-7098
www.craftsreport.com

Threads
63 South Main Street
P.O. Box 5506
Newtown, CT 06470
(800) 477-8727
www.taunton.com

Shows/Events

American Art Marketing
P.O. Box 480
Slate Hill, NY 10973
www.americancraftmarketing.com
(800) 834-9437
Organizers of the MasterWorks
Art and Design Fair at Hancock
Shaker Village

American Craft Council
72 Spring Street, 6th floor
New York, NY 10012
(800) 836-3470
www.craftcouncil.org

AMC, Inc. / AMERICAS-
MART®-ATLANTA
240 Peachtree Street, NW,
suite 2200
Atlanta, GA 30303
www.americasmart.com
(404) 220-3000
Organizers of the Atlanta
International Gift & Home
Furnishings Market

Brimfield Antique Show
Brimfield, MA (need zip code)
www.brimfieldshow.com
There is no one organizer for
this famous show; check the
Web site for a list of promoters.

GLM Shows/George Little
Management, LLC
10 Bank Street
White Plains, NY 10606
www.glmshows.com
(914) 421-3200
Organizers of the National
Stationary Show and other
wholesale gift shows

Round Top Antiques Fair
Round Top Chamber of
Commerce
102 East Mill Street,
P.O. Box 216
Round Top, TX 78954
(979) 249-4042
www.roundtop.org

Stella Show Management
151 West 25th Street, suite 2
New York, NY 10001
www.stellashows.com
(212) 255-0020;
Antiques, art, and collectibles

The Rosen Group
3000 Chestnut Avenue,
suite 304
Baltimore, MD 21211
www.americancraft.com
(410) 889-2933
Organizers of the Buyers Market
of American Craft, Philadelphia

SOFA
The International Exhibition of
Sculptural Objects and
Functional Art, New York and
Chicago
www.sofaexpo.com
(800) 563-7632 or
(773) 506-8860

Wendy Shows
P.O. Box 707
Rye, NY 10580
www.wendyshows.com
(914) 698-3442
Organizer of some of the Park
Avenue Seventh Regiment
Armory shows

Web sites

Another Girl At Play
www.anothergirlatplay.com
Web site and discussion list on
fostering creativity

Jeweler's Resource Bureau
www.jewelersresource.com
An online publication for the
jewelry design community

Ladies Who Launch
www.ladieswholaunch.com
Web site, e-mail newsletter,
and one-day conferences on
starting your own business

Market Research.com
www.marketresearch.com
A continuously updated
collection of market research

Switchboards: Connecting
Creative Women in Business
theswitchboards.com/forum/ind
ex.php
Online discussion boards

Traditional Folk Art
www.traditionalfolkart.com
Artists and crafts show listings

PHOTO CREDITS

Page 1 left: Alan Shortall; Page
1 right: Susan Gentry
McWhinney; Page 2 left:
Michael Weschler; Page 2
middle: Brooke Slezak; Page 2
right: Keith Scott Morton; Page
6 left: Natasha Milne; Page 6
middle: Courtesy of Allen's
19th Century Folkart Gallery,
Palatine Bridge, N.Y; Page 6
right: Andrew McCaul; Page 7
left: Evan Sklar; Page 7 middle:
Colin McGuire; Page 7 right:
Ryan Benyi; Pages 8-13:
Hannah Carpentier; Pages 14-
18: Jim Bastardo; Pages 19, 21:
Andrew McCaul; Page 22:
Evan Sklar; Pages 23, 24:
Alexandra Rowley; Page 26:
Rose Callahan; Pages 27-30:
Jim Bastardo; Page 31: Jay
York/Affordable Photo; Page
32: Courtesy of Allen's 19th
Century Folkart Gallery,
Palatine Bridge, N.Y; Pages 33,
35 left: Andrew McCaul; Page
35 right, 36: Courtesy of
Allen's 19th Century Folkart
Gallery, Palatine Bridge, N.Y;
Pages 37-40: Hannah Gray;
Page 41: Angela Bonavita;
Pages 42-44: Michelle Joy; Page
45: Susan Gentry McWhinney;
Page 46: Zac Williams from
French Inspired Jewelry;
Published by Lark
Books/Sterling Publishing Co.,
Inc.; Pages 49, 50: Michael
Weschler; Pages 51-55: Susan
Gentry McWhinney; Page 56
left: Jack Thompson; Page 56
middle: Lesley Arlasky/Just Me
Photography; Page 56 right:
Nicolas van Krijdt; Page 57
left: Ryan Benyi; Page 57
middle: Thayer Allyson
Gowdy; Page 57 right: David
Butler; Page 58: Colin
McGuire; Pages 59-61: David
Butler; Page 62: Andrew
McCaul; Page 63: David Butler;
Pages 64-67: Andrew McCaul;
Pages 68–71: Nicolas van
Krijdt; Page 71 bottom left:
Andrew McCaul; Page 72:
Nicolas van Krijdt; Pages 73,
75: Andrew McCaul; Page 76-
79: Michael Luppino; Pages 80-
85: Natasha Milne; Page 86:
Andrew McCaul; Pages 87, 89
top: Joe Pallen; Pages 89
bottom, 90: Ron Giusti; Pages
91-95: Ryan Benyi; Pages 96,
97, 99: John Rawlston; Page 99
bottom left: Andrew McCaul;
Page 100: John Rawlston; Pages
101-104: Thayer Allyson
Gowdy; Pages 106-109: Lesley
Arlasky/Just Me Photography;
Page 109 bottom left: Alan
Shortall; Page 110: Lesley
Arlasky/Just Me Photography;
Page 111: Brooke Slezak; Page
112: Jack Thompson; Page 114:
Brooke Slezak; Page 116:
Patrisha McLean; Page 117-
119: Keith Scott Morton; Page
120: Superieur Photographics;
Pages 121-124: Keith Scott
Morton; Page 125: Courtesy of
Marki McMillan and Rae Lynn
White; Pages 126-130: Keith
Scott Morton; Pages 131, 132:
Richard W. Brown; Page 134
top left and right, bottom left:
Eric Roth; Page 134 bottom
right: Richard W. Brown; Page
136 Jerome Perlinghi; Pages
137, 139 top left: Christie
Weller; Page 139 top right:
Courtesy of a friend of Come
Flea with Me; Page 139 bottom
left and right: Christie Weller;
Pages 141-144: Keith Scott
Morton; Page 146 left: Susan
Gentry McWhinney; Page 146
middle: Keith Scott Morton;
Page 146 right: Eric Roth; Page
147 left and middle: Andrew
McCaul. Page 147 right:
Natasha Milne.

INDEX